sauces

sauces

the magic of sauce

Imagine a world without sauce. There'd be no gravy for roasts, no pesto for pasta and, minus the vinegary kick of a salad dressing, lettuce would be a bland proposition indeed. Take away the zing of salsa, the tang of garlic-rich aïoli and the piquant hit of an unctuous horseradish cream, and dining is dull. Sauces add finesse. They finish a dish, offering up flavours and textures that complement what's already on the plate. They elevate good, easy food (a chargrilled steak, a leafy salad, a warming pudding, for instance) into a memorable meal. Whether an uncomplicated affair (a pile of berries reduced to a suave purée at the flick of a processor switch) or a somewhat more ambitious, simmered-for-hours concoction, the rewards of sauce-making are great. Quite simply, with sauce, the dining table is a far more interesting place to be.

Sauces are universal, traversing cultures and climates; they come to us from the four corners of the globe. We've the French to thank for sophisticated emulsions (think of opulent hollandaise or the cool, velvet touch of mayonnaise), useful roux (impossible to make classic macaroni cheese or lobster mornay without one of these) and the lush cream- and butter-based substances that spoon perfectly over fish or chicken. Greece offers up skordalia, a tantalizing amalgam of garlic, mashed potato and aromatic olive oil while Mexico has given the world rustic, punchy salsas. Pungent flavours (chilli, soy and fish sauces, exotic spices and herbs) spike myriad combinations from South East Asia, and what would one possibly serve with roast turkey had the New World not shared its cranberry sauce?

Sauce-making has suffered the reputation of being a tricky culinary discipline to master, but really, this is undeserved. Very little is needed in the way of special equipment, and modern kitchen devices have minimized the slog involved in puréeing, sieving and emulsifying by hand. Required skills run to basic whisking, stirring and skimming and, occasionally, the exertion of a little patience. The rewards of expanding one's sauce repertoire are great; sauces, fundamentally, are quite delicious things. 'A well-made sauce will make even an elephant or a grandfather palatable,' quipped one nineteenth century wag; and while this theory doesn't beg testing, it is true that a sauce, whether it is smooth and silky or thick and chunky, will elevate even everyday dishes to memorable, impressive feasts.

contents

serving chart

The following is an easy-to-read chart showing which sauces are traditionally served with which foods. This, of course, is simply a guide... there might be people who secretly eat their pasta with gravy, their Christmas pudding with butterscotch sauce, or their toast with pineapple salsa, but these are our suggestions.

BEEF

Pan-fried, grilled or barbecued steak	Green peppercorn • Tomato pasta • Demi-glace • Leek and pine nut • Creamy mushroom • Gravy • Pawpaw • Bearnaise • Black bean • Spicy roasted pumpkin and red capsicum • Rocket salsa verde • Tomato and red chilli • Roasted cashew satay Barbecue • Skordalia • Almond and red capsicum • Roasted red capsicum • Japanese soy, mirin and sesame • Chunky roasted red onion
Roast	Gravy • Bearnaise • Tomato and red chilli
Corned beef	Classic white (béchamel)
Cold meats	Cumberland • Sour cherry • Champagne apple
Sausages	Barbecue • Roasted cashew satay • Roasted red capsicum
Hamburgers	Barbecue • Roasted cashew satay • Roasted red capsicum

LAMB

Pan-fried, grilled chops or fillets	Pawpaw • Spiced coconut • Black bean • Almond and red capsicum • Spicy pumpkin and red capsicum • Leek and pine nut Skordalia • Sweet and sour • Roasted red onion • Roasted red capsicum • Tomato and red chilli
Roast	Gravy • Mint

PORK

Pan-fried, grilled or barbecued	Sweet and sour • Apple • Pawpaw • Black bean • Champagne apple • Roasted cashew satay
Roast	Cranberry • Apple • Gravy • Sour cherry • Champagne apple
Ham	Cumberland • Sour cherry • Champagne apple

VEAL

Pan-fried	Velouté • Tomato pasta • Creamy mushroom • Leek and pine nut Chunky roasted red onion • Tomato and chilli Roasted red capsicum

GAME Sour cherry • Gravy

PASTA Bolognese • Tomato pasta • Pesto • Almond and red capsicum • Roasted walnut Leek and pine nut • Rocket salsa verde

CHICKEN/TURKEY

Pan-fried, barbecued or grilled	Green peppercorn • Cumberland • Satay • Hollandaise • Skordalia • Creamy mushroom • Mint and yoghurt • Champagne apple Almond and red capsicum • Leek and pine nut • Rocket salsa verde • Tomato and red chilli • Black bean • Sour cherry • Chinese lemon • Bombay lime • Velouté • Roasted cashew satay • Pawpaw • Pesto • Roasted red capsicum
Roast	Cranberry • Gravy • Bread

SEAFOOD
SHELLFISH

Prawns, Lobster, Crab	Skordalia • Blue cheese, pecan and cognac grilling sauce • Cheese (mornay) Bombay lime
Oysters, mussels	Almond and red capsicum • Black bean • Cheese (mornay) • Velouté
Scallops	Japanese soy, mirin and sesame • Velouté • Beurre blanc Bombay lime

SALMON

Pan-fried steaks	Sweet and sour • Satay • Beurre blanc
Poached whole or fillets	Hollandaise • Sorrel and lemon • Bearnaise • Bombay lime Leek and pinenut

TUNA

Pan-fried or barbecued steaks	Almond and red capsicum • Spicy roasted pumpkin and red capsicum • Chilli spiced mango Bombay lime • Beurre blanc

WHITE FILLETS

Pan-fried, grilled, barbecued or deep-fried	Satay • Rocket salsa verde • Sweet and sour • Satay • Gazpacho • Pesto • Spiced coconut Pesto • Spiced coconut • Bombay lime • Velouté • Beurre blanc

WHOLE FISH

baked, pan-fried or barbecued	Chilli spiced mango • Tomato and red chilli • Sorrel and lemon • Chinese lemon • Veloute Classic white (béchamel) • Cheese (mornay)

VEGETABLES

Artichokes	Beurre blanc • Bombay lime
Asparagus	Hollandaise • Gazpacho • Beurre blanc • Bombay lime
Eggplant	Skordalia
Broccoli	Classic white (béchamel)
Cauliflower	Classic white (béchamel)
Potatoes	Gravy • Leek and pine nut • Spicy roasted pumpkin and red capsicum
Tomatoes	Pesto
Grilled, steamed , boiled	Roasted red capsicum • Japanese soy, mirin and sesame • Beurre blanc • Roasted walnut Hollandaise • Japanese soy, mirin and sesame • Cheese (mornay) • Spiced coconut • Tomato and red chilli Chinese lemon • Beurre blanc • Skordalia

DESSERTS

Fresh Fruit	Iced orange • Burnt sugar • Praline cream • Brandy cream • Chocolate rum • Berry coulis
Poached fruit	Zabaglione • Burnt sugar • Coconut lime anglaise • Praline cream • Hot chocolate • Brandy cream • Butterscotch • Berry coulis
Ice cream	Burnt sugar • Chocolate rum • Berry coulis
Pancakes/Waffles	Iced orange • Burnt sugar • Praline cream • Hot chocolate • Butterscotch • Chocolate rum
Steamed puddings	Vanilla custard • Coconut lime anglaise • Hot chocolate • Brandy cream • Butterscotch Chocolate rum
Fruit pies and tarts	Vanilla custard • Coconut lime anglaise • Brandy cream • Berry coulis • Crème anglaise

savoury sauces

aïoli (garlic mayonnaise)

serves 6

6 garlic cloves

2 egg yolks

250 ml (9 fl oz/1 cup) olive oil

lemon juice, optional

Serve with salads, egg dishes, fish soup or cold poached fish. Also good with vegetables.

1 Blend the garlic cloves, egg yolks and a pinch of salt in a blender until a thick paste forms.

2 With the motor running, add the olive oil, drop by drop, until the aïoli is thick and creamy. If it becomes too thick, add a little lemon juice. Season to taste. This recipe can also be made using a mortar and pestle.

almond and red capsicum sauce

serves 6

Serve with lamb cutlets or steaks.

1 large red capsicum (pepper), seeded and quartered

2 garlic cloves, unpeeled

125 g (4$^1/_2$ oz/1$^1/_3$ cups) flaked almonds

80 ml (2$^1/_2$ fl oz/$^1/_3$ cup) red wine vinegar

170 ml (5$^1/_2$ fl oz/$^2/_3$ cup) olive oil

60 ml (2 fl oz/$^1/_4$ cup) boiling water

2 tablespoons finely chopped parsley

1 Cook the capsicum, skin side up, under a hot grill (broiler) for 10 minutes. Add the garlic and cook until the capsicum skin blackens and blisters. Cool the garlic and capsicum in a plastic bag, then peel away the skin.

2 Spread the almonds on a baking tray and roast under a moderate grill, stirring once or twice, until lightly golden. Set aside to cool for 5 minutes.

3 Process the peeled capsicum, garlic and almonds in a food processor until smooth. With the motor running, slowly add the vinegar. Season with salt and pepper. Gradually add the oil, then the boiling water. The sauce should have the consistency of mayonnaise. Add the parsley and process briefly. Refrigerate the sauce overnight before serving.

anchovy and rosemary sauce

serves 4

8 large anchovy fillets, chopped

3 teaspoons finely chopped rosemary leaves

150 ml (5 1/2 fl oz) olive oil

1 tablespoon lemon juice

To serve, slice the lamb fillets into four pieces on the diagonal, cutting across the grain. Put the grilled polenta on warmed serving plates, top it with the lamb and rocket and drizzle with the sauce.

1 Put the anchovies and rosemary in a food processor and blend them to a paste. Add the olive oil in a thin stream, then add the lemon juice and season with salt and pepper.

2 Preheat a barbecue chargrill plate to medium direct heat. Grill the polenta squares for 7–8 minutes on each side or until they are crisp and golden. When the polenta is ready, move the squares to the side of the grill, season the lamb fillets with salt and cook for 2–3 minutes each side for medium– rare, or until cooked to your liking.

balsamic vinaigrette

serves 6

**2 tablespoons
balsamic vinegar**

1 teaspoon Dijon mustard

**80 ml (2¹/₂ fl oz/¹/₃ cup)
extra virgin olive oil**

1 small garlic clove

Serve drizzled over a green salad or sliced tomatoes.

1 Whisk the vinegar and mustard in a small bowl until combined. Gradually beat in the olive oil. Season with salt and freshly ground black pepper.

2 Cut the garlic clove in half, skewer onto a toothpick and leave in the dressing to infuse for at least 1 hour.

barbecue sauce

serves 4

2 teaspoons oil

1 small onion,
finely chopped

1 tablespoon malt vinegar

1 tablespoon soft
brown sugar

80 ml (2^1/$_2$ fl oz/^{1}/$_3$ cup)
tomato sauce (ketchup)

1 tablespoon
worcestershire sauce

Serve with hamburgers, barbecued chops,
steaks or sausages.

1 Heat the oil in a small saucepan over low
heat. Cook the onion, stirring occasionally, for
3 minutes, or until soft.

2 Add the vinegar, sugar, tomato sauce and
worcestershire sauce and bring to the boil.
Reduce the heat and simmer, stirring
occasionally, for 3 minutes. Serve warm or
at room temperature.

basil garlic dressing

serves 8

Serve with a green salad.

1 garlic clove

2 tablespoons chopped basil

60 ml (2 fl oz/^{1}/$_4$ cup) lemon juice

125 ml (4 fl oz/^{1}/$_2$ cup) extra virgin olive oil

1 Process the garlic and basil in a food processor or blender until finely chopped.

2 Add the lemon juice and process in short bursts until the mixture is combined. Gradually add the olive oil and process until combined. Season to taste with salt and freshly ground black pepper.

bearnaise sauce

serves 4

80 ml (2¹/₂ fl oz/¹/₃ cup)
white wine vinegar

2 spring onions (scallions),
roughly chopped

2 teaspoons chopped
tarragon

2 egg yolks

125 g (4¹/₂ oz) butter, cubed

Serve with roast beef or lamb,
pan-fried steaks or poached salmon.

1 Put the vinegar, spring onion and tarragon in
a small saucepan. Bring to the boil, then reduce
the heat slightly and simmer until the
mixture has reduced by a third. Set aside to
cool completely.

2 Strain the vinegar into a heatproof bowl and add
the egg yolks. Place the bowl over a saucepan of
barely simmering water and whisk until the
mixture is thick and pale.

3 Add the butter, one cube at a time, and whisk
after each addition until the mixture is thick and
smooth. Season to taste and serve immediately.

Boil the vinegar with the onions
and tarragon to give flavour, then
strain.

Place the bowl over a pan of
simmering water so the mixture
doesn't overheat.

Add the butter a cube at a time,
whisking well after each addition.

béchamel (white sauce)

serves 4

250 ml (9 fl oz/1 cup) milk
1 slice of onion
1 bay leaf
6 peppercorns
30 g (1 oz) butter
1 tablespoon plain
(all-purpose) flour
freshly ground white pepper

Serve with fish, corned beef, steamed cauliflower or steamed broccoli.

1 Put the milk, onion, bay leaf and peppercorns in a small saucepan. Bring to the boil, then remove from the heat. Set aside to infuse for 10 minutes, then strain the milk.

2 Melt the butter in a small saucepan and add the flour. Cook, stirring, for 1 minute, or until the mixture is golden and bubbling. Remove from the heat and gradually add the milk, stirring after each addition until completely smooth.

3 Return to the heat and stir until the mixture boils. Continue cooking for 1 minute, or until thick. Season with salt and white pepper. Serve hot.

To add flavour to the milk, infuse with the onion, bay leaf and peppercorns.

Cook the flour and butter, stirring all the time, until golden and bubbling.

After adding the milk, return the pan to the heat and continue stirring to remove any lumps.

beurre blanc

serves 4

2 French shallots, chopped

60 ml (2 fl oz/¼ cup) white wine vinegar

220 g (7¾ oz) unsalted butter, cubed

lemon juice, to taste

Serve with seafood, steamed artichoke hearts or steamed or boiled vegetables.

1 Put the shallots, vinegar and 60 ml (2 fl oz/¼ cup) of water in a saucepan. Bring to the boil, then reduce the heat and simmer until the mixture is reduced to 2 tablespoons. Strain into a clean saucepan and return to low heat.

2 Whisk in the butter, a few pieces at a time. The sauce will thicken as the butter is added until it is the consistency of cream. Season to taste with salt, pepper and lemon juice and serve warm.

Note: If the sauce is too hot, the butter will separate; too cold and it will set. Keep it warm in a bowl over a saucepan of gently simmering water.

Chop the French shallots, then simmer in the vinegar and water until reduced.

Strain the reduced mixture into a clean pan, discarding the chopped shallot.

Whisk the butter into the mixture, a few cubes at a time.

blackcurrant sauce

serves 6

Serve over grilled (broiled) duck breasts.

500 ml (17 fl oz/2 cups)
red wine

55 g (2 oz/^{1}/$_4$ cup) sugar

200 g (7 oz/1^2/$_3$ cups)
blackcurrants

1 tablespoon red
wine vinegar

1 Put the red wine in a saucepan and bring to the boil. Add the sugar and cook until the mixture has reduced by half.

2 Add the blackcurrants and vinegar and simmer until the blackcurrants are tender. Serve hot.

black bean sauce

serves 6

Serve with stir-fried meat or chicken, prawns (shrimp), scallops or crab.

2 tablespoons salted black beans

1 tablespoon vegetable oil

1 small onion, finely chopped

1 garlic clove, finely chopped

1 tablespoon finely chopped fresh ginger

1 red chilli, seeded and finely chopped

310 ml (10³/4 fl oz/1¹/4 cups) chicken stock

2 teaspoons cornflour (cornstarch)

2 teaspoons sesame oil

1 Rinse the black beans under cold water for 3–4 minutes to remove any excess salt. Drain well.

2 Heat the vegetable oil in a small saucepan over low heat. Add the onion, garlic, ginger and chilli and cook until the onion is soft but not browned. Add the stock and bring to the boil. Reduce the heat and simmer for 5 minutes.

3 Mix the cornflour with 1 tablespoon of water. Add to the sauce and cook, stirring, until the sauce has thickened. Simmer for 3 minutes, then add the black beans and sesame oil and mix well. Serve hot.

Rinse the black beans under running water to get rid of excess saltiness.

Cook until the onion is soft but not browned, then add the stock.

Simmer the sauce for 3 minutes, then stir in the beans and sesame oil.

black sesame dressing

serves 4–6

50 g (1³/4 oz/¹/3 cup) black sesame seeds

1¹/2 teaspoons caster (superfine) sugar

1 tablespoon sake

1¹/2 tablespoons dashi (see note)

2 teaspoons tamari

Serve with blanched or steamed English spinach, pasta or steamed vegetables.

1 Put the sesame seeds in a dry frying pan and fry over medium heat, stirring regularly, for about 5 minutes, or until aromatic. Immediately transfer the sesame seeds to a mortar.

2 Grind the sesame seeds until very finely crushed. Gradually incorporate the sugar, sake, dashi and tamari until the mixture forms a smooth paste.

Note: To make the dashi, dissolve ¹/4 teaspoon of instant dashi granules in 125 ml (4 fl oz/¹/2 cup) of boiling water and stir until dissolved.

blue cheese dressing

serves 6–8

125 g (4^1/$_2$ oz/^{1}/$_2$ cup) whole-egg mayonnaise

60 ml (2 fl oz/^{1}/$_4$ cup) thick (double/heavy) cream

1 teaspoon white wine vinegar

1 tablespoon finely snipped chives

50 g (1^3/$_4$ oz) blue cheese

freshly ground white pepper

Serve over asparagus, boiled new potatoes or jacket potatoes, or with a green salad.

1 Combine the mayonnaise, cream, vinegar and chives in a small bowl.

2 Crumble the blue cheese into the mayonnaise mixture and gently stir to combine. Season to taste with salt and freshly ground white pepper.

blue cheese sauce

serves 4

Serve over boiled new potatoes or jacket potatoes, or gnocchi.

90 g (3^1/$_4$ oz) blue cheese

160 ml (^{2}/$_3$ cup) cream

1 Put the blue cheese and cream in a saucepan and gently heat them together until smooth.

2 Pour the blue cheese sauce over the cooked pasta or potatoes.

blueberry and mint vinegar

makes 750 ml (26 fl oz)

500 ml (17 fl oz/2 cups)
white wine vinegar

310 g (11 oz/2 cups)
blueberries

8 mint sprigs

Use in place of white wine vinegar for a flavoured vinaigrette.

1 Put the vinegar, blueberries and half the mint sprigs in a saucepan. Bring to the boil, then reduce the heat and simmer for 5 minutes. Remove from the heat.

2 Discard the mint sprigs and pour the mixture into a warm sterilized jar. Add the remaining mint sprigs, seal and store in the fridge for a week.

3 Line a funnel with muslin and strain the vinegar into warm sterilized bottles. Seal and label. Store for up to a year.

bread sauce

serves 4

Serve with roast chicken, turkey, goose or game.

2 whole cloves

1 onion, peeled

250 ml (9 fl oz/1 cup) milk

1 bay leaf

55 g (2 oz/²/₃ cup) fresh breadcrumbs

60 ml (2 fl oz/¹/₄ cup) cream (whipping)

1 Push the cloves into the onion and put in a saucepan with the milk and bay leaf. Bring to the boil, then remove from the heat, cover and set aside for 10 minutes. Discard the onion and bay leaf.

2 Add the breadcrumbs to the milk and season. Return to the heat, cover and simmer gently, stirring occasionally, for 10 minutes. Stir in the cream. Serve warm.

Stud the onion with the whole cloves to add flavour to the milk.

Once the milk has infused for 10 minutes lift out the onion and bay leaf.

Stir in the fresh breadcrumbs and then return the pan to the heat.

caesar dressing

serves 6

Serve on Caesar salad or any other green salad.

1 egg

2 teaspoons white wine vinegar

3 teaspoons Dijon mustard

1 anchovy fillet

1 garlic clove, crushed

80 ml (2¹/₂ fl oz/¹/₃ cup) oil

1 Lower the egg into a saucepan of boiling water. Cook for 1 minute, then drain.

2 Break the egg into a small bowl. Add the vinegar, mustard, anchovy and garlic and whisk to combine.

3 Add the oil in a thin stream, whisking continuously, until the mixture is smooth and creamy.

calvados gravy

serves 8

Serve with roast pork.

pan juices from roast pork

1 tablespoon Calvados

2 tablespoons plain (all-purpose) flour

375 ml (13 fl oz/1 1/2 cups) chicken stock

125 ml (4 fl oz/1/2 cup) unsweetened apple juice

1 Drain off all but 2 tablespoons of the pan juices from the roasting tin. Place the tin on the stove over medium heat. Stir in the Calvados and cook for 1 minute.

2 Remove from the heat, stir in the flour and mix well. Return to the heat and cook, stirring, for 2 minutes. Gradually add the stock and apple juice and cook, stirring, until the gravy has thickened. Season to taste. Serve hot.

caper sauce

Serve with veal schnitzel or tuna steaks.

30 g (1 oz) butter

30 g (1 oz/¼ cup) plain (all-purpose) flour

150 ml (5 fl oz) lukewarm milk

150 ml (5 fl oz) lukewarm beef stock

1 tablespoon capers, rinsed and squeezed dry

1–2 teaspoons lemon juice

freshly ground white pepper

1 Melt the butter in a small saucepan, then blend in the flour. Cook, whisking continuously, for 1 minute.

2 Remove from the heat and gradually whisk in the milk and stock. Return to the heat and slowly bring to the boil, whisking until the mixture boils and thickens. Reduce the heat and simmer very gently for 2–3 minutes.

3 Add the capers and lemon juice, to taste. Season with salt and white pepper. Serve hot.

caramelized onion sauce

serves 4–6

40 g (1¹/₂ oz) butter

3 onions, sliced

1 tablespoon plain
(all-purpose) flour

375 ml (13 fl oz/1¹/₂ cups)
beef stock

1 tablespoon red wine
vinegar

Serve with steaks or sausages or
on hamburgers.

1 Melt the butter in a large saucepan over low
   heat. Add the onion and cook for 30 minutes, or
   until soft and brown. Add the flour and cook,
   stirring constantly, for 1 minute.

2 Gradually add the stock, stirring constantly until
   combined. Stir in the vinegar and bring to the
   boil. Reduce the heat and simmer for 2 minutes.
   Serve hot or warm.

champagne apple sauce

serves 6–8

185 ml (6 fl oz/³/4 cup) Champagne or sparkling white wine

4 green apples, peeled, cored and chopped

¹/2 teaspoon finely grated lemon zest

1 tablespoon finely chopped lemon thyme or thyme

40 g (1¹/2 oz) butter, cubed

Serve with roast pork, pan-fried pork chops, a whole roast ham or turkey.

1 Pour the wine into a saucepan and boil for 1 minute. Add the apple and lemon zest, cover and simmer for 10 minutes, or until the apple is tender. Stir in the lemon thyme and set aside to cool for 5 minutes.

2 Purée the apple mixture in a food processor. Gradually add the butter, processing after each addition. Season to taste with salt and pepper. Serve warm or at room temperature.

Peel the apples, remove the cores and chop the flesh.

Simmer the apple and lemon rind until the apple is tender. Add the lemon thyme.

Add the butter gradually, processing after each addition.

chargrilled vegetable salsa

serves 4

2 Roma (plum) tomatoes, halved lengthways

1 small red capsicum (pepper), seeded and halved lengthways

1 small green capsicum (pepper), seeded and halved lengthways

2 small zucchini (courgettes), halved lengthways

2 long thin eggplants (aubergines), halved lengthways

60 ml (2 fl oz/¼ cup) olive oil

2 teaspoons chopped oregano

2 tablespoons chopped flat-leaf (Italian) parsley

1 tablespoon chopped marjoram

2 tablespoons balsamic vinegar

Serve with barbecued or grilled (broiled) meat or chicken.

1 Place the vegetables in a large shallow dish. Combine the oil with the oregano, half the parsley and half the marjoram. Pour over the vegetables, toss well and set aside to marinate for at least 2 hours.

2 Heat a barbecue or chargrill pan and cook the vegetables until soft and a little blackened. Cool the capsicum in a plastic bag for a few minutes, then peel. Chop all the vegetables into small pieces and mix with the balsamic vinegar and remaining parsley and marjoram. Serve warm.

chunky roasted red onion sauce

serves 6–8

500 g (1 lb 2 oz) red onions, thinly sliced

1 kg (2 lb 4 oz) baby onions

3 large garlic cloves

2 tablespoons olive oil

1.5 kg (3 lb 5 oz) Roma (plum) tomatoes, halved lengthways

1 teaspoon salt

3 tablespoons chopped oregano

440 g (15 1/2 oz) tin tomatoes, roughly chopped

1 tablespoon muscatel liqueur or brandy

1 tablespoon soft brown sugar

Serve with barbecued steaks and mashed potatoes.

1   Preheat the oven to 200°C (400°F/Gas 6). Put the red onions, baby onions and garlic in a large roasting tin with half the oil. Roll the onions in the oil so that they are lightly coated. Add the Roma tomatoes, drizzle with the remaining oil and sprinkle with the salt and oregano. Roast for 1 hour.

2   Spoon the chopped tomatoes and juice into the roasting tin, taking care not to break up the roasted tomatoes. Drizzle the muscatel or brandy over the top and sprinkle with the brown sugar. Roast for 20 minutes. Serve hot.

chilli barbecue sauce

serves 4–6

20 g (3/4 oz) butter

1 teaspoon ground cumin

1/2 teaspoon ground coriander

1/2 teaspoon paprika

80 ml (21/2 fl oz/1/3 cup) ready-made barbecue sauce

1 tablespoon sweet chilli sauce

2 teaspoons worcestershire sauce

Serve with barbecued lamb, beef or hamburgers.

1 Heat the butter in a small saucepan over low–medium heat. Add the cumin, coriander and paprika and cook for 30 seconds.

2 Add the barbecue sauce, sweet chilli sauce and worcestershire sauce and mix well. Serve warm.

chunky tomato sauce

serves 4

1.5 kg (3 lb 5 oz) tomatoes

1 tablespoon olive oil

1 onion, finely chopped

2 garlic cloves, crushed

2 tablespoons tomato paste
(concentrated purée)

1 teaspoon dried oregano

1 teaspoon sugar

Serve hot with pasta, pan-fried steaks or veal schnitzel, or cool and use as a sauce for pizza bases.

1   Score a cross in the base of each tomato. Place in a heatproof bowl and cover with boiling water. Set aside for 30 seconds, then transfer to cold water and peel the skin away from the cross. Finely chop the tomatoes.

2   Heat the oil in a saucepan over medium heat. Add the onion, stirring, for 3 minutes, or until soft. Add the garlic and cook for 1 minute.

3   Add the tomatoes, tomato paste, oregano and sugar. Bring to the boil, then reduce the heat and simmer for 20 minutes, or until the sauce has thickened slightly. Season to taste.

chilli dipping sauce

serves 4–6

1 tablespoon peanut oil

1 garlic clove, crushed

60 ml (2 fl oz/¼ cup) sweet chilli sauce

2 tablespoons soy sauce

2 tablespoons sherry

1 tablespoon lemon juice

Serve with Thai starters such as spring rolls and fish cakes.

1 Heat the oil in a small saucepan over medium heat. Add the garlic until just golden.

2 Add the sweet chilli sauce, soy sauce, sherry and lemon juice and stir until smooth and heated through. Serve warm.

chilli lime dressing

serves 6–8

60 ml (2 fl oz/¼ cup)
lime juice

2 tablespoons fish sauce

1–2 teaspoons sambal oelek
(chilli paste)

1 teaspoon sugar

60 ml (2 fl oz/¼ cup) oil

Serve with chargrilled prawns (shrimp) or stir-fried Asian greens.

1 Combine the lime juice, fish sauce, sambal oelek and sugar in a small bowl.

2 Using a small wire whisk or fork, gradually whisk in the oil in a thin stream until well blended.

chinese lemon sauce

60 ml (2 fl oz/¼ cup)
lemon juice

60 ml (2 fl oz/¼ cup)
chicken stock

1 tablespoon honey

1 tablespoon sugar

½ teaspoon grated
fresh ginger

1 tablespoon cornflour
(cornstarch)

2 spring onions (scallions),
sliced on the diagonal

a few drops of sesame oil

Serve with deep-fried won tons, spring rolls and dumplings. Also good with vegetables, chicken or fish.

1 Put the lemon juice, stock, honey, sugar and ginger in a saucepan with 125 ml (4 fl oz/½ cup) of water. Stir over medium heat until the sugar has dissolved.

2 Increase the heat and bring to the boil. Blend the cornflour with a little water and add to the pan, stirring constantly until the sauce boils and thickens. Remove from the heat, stir in the spring onions and season with salt. Drizzle with the sesame oil and serve warm.

coriander and lime cream

serves 4

Serve with salmon.

1 large handful coriander (cilantro) leaves

2 tablespoons chopped coriander (cilantro) stems

grated zest of 1 lime

1 tablespoon lime juice

150 g (5^1/$_2$ oz/^{2}/$_3$ cup) crème fraîche or sour cream

1 Put the coriander leaves and stems, lime zest, lime juice and crème fraîche or sour cream in a blender or small processor fitted with the metal blade. Whizz for 35–50 seconds, or until the mixture is creamy.

2 The cream can be made in advance and chilled in an airtight container for up to 45 minutes before use. It will change texture if left any longer.

corn and chilli salsa

serves 4

175 g (6 oz/2 bunches)
coriander (cilantro)

2 garlic cloves, crushed

50 g (1³/4 oz/¹/3 cup) roasted
macadamia nuts

1 teaspoon chopped
red chilli

80 ml (2¹/2 fl oz/¹/3 cup)
olive oil

Serve with pasta, grilled (broiled) fish or chicken.

1   Trim the roots from the coriander, leaving most
of the stems. Wash and dry the stems.

2   Process the coriander, garlic, macadamia nuts
and chilli in a food processor until finely
chopped. With the motor running, add the
oil in a thin stream until well combined. Season
to taste.

cranberry sauce

serves 6–8

Serve with roast turkey, chicken or pork.

1 orange

500 g (1 lb 2 oz/4 cups) fresh or frozen cranberries

110 g (3¾ oz/¹/₂ cup) sugar

125 ml (4 fl oz/¹/₂ cup) orange juice

2 tablespoons port

1 cinnamon stick

1 Peel the orange and cut the zest into thick strips, removing all the white pith.

2 Put the cranberries, sugar, orange juice, orange zest, port and cinnamon stick in a heavy-based saucepan. Bring to the boil, then reduce the heat and simmer for 5 minutes. Remove from the heat.

3 Remove the orange zest and cinnamon stick, including any small pieces that have broken away. Set aside to cool before serving.

creamy horseradish sauce

serves 8–10

175 g (6 oz/¹/₂ cup)
horseradish cream

1 bulb spring onion
(scallion), finely chopped

60 g (2¹/₄ oz/¹/₄ cup)
sour cream

125 ml (4 fl oz/¹/₂ cup)
cream (whipping)

Serve with roast beef, smoked salmon or vegetable crudités.

1 Combine the horseradish cream, spring onion and sour cream in a small bowl.

2 Whip the cream until soft peaks form. Fold the cream into the horseradish mixture. Season to taste.

creamy mushroom sauce

serves 4

Serve over pan-fried beef steaks, veal steaks or boneless, skinless chicken breasts.

30 g (1 oz) butter

pan juices from pan-fried beef, veal or chicken

350 g (12 oz/4^1/3 cups) button mushrooms, sliced

2 tablespoons white wine

125 ml (4 fl oz/^{1}/2 cup) chicken stock

125 ml (4 fl oz/^{1}/2 cup) cream (whipping)

1 garlic clove, crushed

1 tablespoon chopped chives

1 Melt the butter in the frying pan containing the pan juices over medium heat, add the mushrooms and stir for 5 minutes, or until the mushrooms are soft and golden.

2 Add the wine, stock, cream and garlic and bring to the boil. Cook, stirring constantly, for 2 minutes, or until the sauce has thickened slightly. Add the chives and serve immediately.

Chop the chives into short, even lengths with a sharp knife.

Add the butter and sliced mushrooms to the pan juices and cook until golden.

Add the wine, stock, cream and garlic, and bring to the boil.

cucumber dipping sauce

serves 6-8

Serve with Thai starters such as spring rolls and fish cakes.

1/2 Lebanese (short) cucumber, roughly chopped

1/2 carrot, chopped

2 spring onions (scallions), roughly chopped

1 small red chilli, seeded and chopped

1 teaspoon grated fresh ginger

1 tablespoon roasted unsalted peanuts

1 tablespoon chopped coriander (cilantro)

80 g (2^3/$_4$ oz/^{1}/$_3$ cup) caster (superfine) sugar

185 ml (6 fl oz/^{3}/$_4$ cup) white wine vinegar or rice vinegar

1   Briefly process the cucumber, carrot, spring onion, chilli, ginger, peanuts and coriander in a food processor until finely chopped, being careful not to overprocess the mixture. Transfer to a serving bowl.

2   Heat the sugar, vinegar and 60 ml (2 fl oz/^{1}/$_4$ cup) of water in a small saucepan. Stir until the sugar has dissolved, then pour over the cucumber mixture. Serve warm or cold.

cumberland sauce

Serve this traditional sauce cold with ham, turkey, venison or game.

2 oranges

1 lemon

225 g (8 oz/³/₄ cup) redcurrant jelly

2 teaspoons Dijon mustard

2 tablespoons red wine vinegar

250 ml (9 fl oz/1 cup) port

1 Remove the orange and lemon zest with a zester. Place the zest in a small saucepan with 250 ml (9 fl oz/1 cup) of water and bring to the boil. Cook for 5 minutes, then strain the liquid, reserving the zest.

2 Squeeze the juice from the oranges and lemon and pour into a saucepan. Add the redcurrant jelly, mustard, vinegar, port and reserved citrus zest. Slowly bring to the boil, stirring as the jelly melts. Reduce the heat and simmer gently for 15 minutes. Season to taste. Serve chilled or at room temperature.

If you don't have a zester, use a small knife to remove the rind from the fruit.

Place the orange and lemon juice in a pan and add the remaining ingredients.

Bring slowly to the boil, stirring as the redcurrant jelly melts.

curry béchamel

250 ml (9 fl oz/1 cup) milk

1 slice of onion

1 bay leaf

6 peppercorns

30 g (1 oz) butter

1 small onion,
finely chopped

2 teaspoons curry powder

1 tablespoon plain
(all-purpose) flour

freshly ground white pepper

Serve over steamed or poached fish.

1 Put the milk, onion slice, bay leaf and peppercorns in a small saucepan. Bring to the boil, then remove from the heat. Set aside to infuse for 10 minutes, then strain the milk.

2 Melt the butter in a small saucepan. Add the onion and curry powder and cook, stirring, for 2 minutes, or until the onion is soft. Add the flour and cook, stirring, for 1 minute, or until the mixture is golden and bubbling.

3 Remove from the heat and gradually add the infused milk, stirring after each addition until completely smooth. Return to the heat and stir until boiling, then cook for 1 minute, or until thick. Season with salt and white pepper. Serve hot.

demi-glace

serves 8

Serve with any type of beef steak.

beef stock

1 kg (2 lb 4 oz) beef bones

1 tablespoon oil

1 onion, chopped

2 carrots, chopped

5 parsley stalks

2 bay leaves

6 peppercorns

espagnole

2 tablespoons oil

2 carrots, finely chopped

1 onion, finely chopped

1 celery stalk,
finely chopped

1 tablespoon plain
(all-purpose) flour

1/2 teaspoon tomato paste
(concentrated purée)

bouquet garni

1 To make the beef stock, preheat the oven to 220°C (425°F/Gas 7). Roast the beef bones for 1 hour, or until browned. Heat the oil in a large saucepan and brown the vegetables, being careful not to burn them. Add the bones, parsley, bay leaves and peppercorns and cover with cold water. Bring to the boil, then reduce the heat and simmer for 3–4 hours, skimming off the fat as it rises to the surface. Add a little more cold water if needed. You should have about 875 ml (30 fl oz/3½ cups) of stock — if you have more, continue reducing; if less, add a little water. Strain and cool. Remove any fat that sets on the surface.

2 To make the espagnole, heat the oil in a saucepan and brown the vegetables. Add the flour and cook, stirring, until browned. Add 625 ml (21½ fl oz/2½ cups) of the beef stock with the tomato paste and bouquet garni and bring to the boil. Reduce the heat, half-cover the pan and simmer, skimming off any fat, for 30 minutes, or until reduced to 250 ml (9 fl oz/1 cup). Strain and set aside to cool.

3 To make the demi-glace, put the espagnole and remaining beef stock in a saucepan and simmer until reduced by half. Strain thoroughly through a fine mesh sieve or muslin. Serve warm.

Note: Don't use ready-made stock as it is far too salty for this recipe. To make a bouquet garni, wrap the green part of a leek around a bay leaf, sprig of thyme, some celery leaves and a few stalks of parsely, then tie with string. To make a beef glace, reduce the strained stock to a thick sticky liquid, which will set to a jelly when cold. This gives a rich flavour when added to sauces.

To make the espagnole, heat the oil in a pan and brown the chopped vegetables.

Half-cover the pan and leave to simmer for 30 minutes, skimming off any fat.

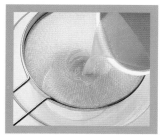

Strain the sauce again through a fine sieve or muslin.

dill mayonnaise

serves 6

185 g (6¹/₂ oz/³/₄ cup)
whole-egg mayonnaise

60 g (2¹/₄ oz/¹/₄ cup)
plain yoghurt

¹/₄ teaspoon finely grated
lemon zest

1¹/₂ tablespoons
chopped dill

1 teaspoon lemon juice

pinch of caster
(superfine) sugar

Serve with baked whole salmon.

1 Put the mayonnaise, yoghurt, lemon zest, dill,
lemon juice and sugar in a bowl and mix to
combine. Season to taste.

2 Cover and refrigerate for 1 hour before serving.

dill sauce

125 g (4^1/$_2$ oz/^{1}/$_2$ cup)
plain yoghurt

125 g (4^1/$_2$ oz/^{1}/$_2$ cup)
sour cream

1 tablespoon horseradish
cream

2 tablespoons chopped dill

3 spring onions (scallions),
finely chopped

Serve with fish, or spoon over steamed new potatoes.

1   Combine the yoghurt, sour cream and horseradish cream in a bowl and stir until creamy.

2   Add the dill and spring onions and mix well. Season with salt and freshly ground black pepper. Serve chilled.

dried apricot sauce

Serve with a vegetarian nut roast.

250 g (9 oz/1$1/3$ cups)
dried apricots

1 cinnamon stick

1 cardamom pod

90 g (3$1/4$ oz/$1/3$ cup) Greek
style yoghurt

1 Put the dried apricots, cinnamon stick and cardamom pod in a saucepan and cover with cold water. Bring to the boil, then reduce the heat and simmer for 15 minutes, or until the apricots are very soft. Set aside to cool.

2 Remove the spices and purée the sauce until smooth, adding more water if needed. Set aside to cool completely.

3 Stir the yoghurt into the sauce and serve.

eggplant, capsicum and olive salsa

serves 6

1 eggplant (aubergine), diced

60 ml (2 fl oz/¼ cup) olive oil

½ teaspoon salt

1 large red capsicum (pepper), seeded and diced

12 kalamata olives, pitted and finely chopped

4 spring onions (scallions), finely chopped

1 small red chilli, chopped

2 garlic cloves, crushed

2 teaspoons red wine vinegar

2 teaspoons lemon juice

1 tablespoon chopped parsley

2 teaspoons snipped chives

Serve with wood-fired bread or barbecued beef, lamb or chicken.

1 Preheat the oven to 180°C (350°F/Gas 4). Toss the eggplant with 2 tablespoons of the olive oil and the salt, then place in a single layer on a baking tray. Roast for 20 minutes, or until golden and cooked. Set aside to cool.

2 Combine the eggplant, capsicum, olives, spring onion, chilli, garlic, vinegar, lemon juice and remaining oil. Season to taste. Add the parsley and chives. Serve at room temperature.

father's favourite sauce

serves 8

5 large tomatoes (1 kg/2 lb 4 oz), chopped

1 large onion, chopped

125 ml (4 fl oz/^{1}/2 cup) cider vinegar

185 g (6^1/2 oz/1 cup) soft brown sugar

60 ml (2 fl oz/^{1}/4 cup) worcestershire sauce

1 teaspoon ground allspice

^{1}/2 teaspoon ground ginger

^{1}/4 teaspoon ground cloves

Serve with sausages, steaks or chops. Also good as a relish with cold meats.

1 Put the tomatoes and onion in a large saucepan. Add the vinegar, sugar, worcestershire sauce and spices. Season with salt and pepper. Bring to the boil, then reduce the heat and simmer, stirring occasionally, for 40 minutes. Transfer to a bowl to cool.

2 Process the sauce in a food processor until almost smooth. Return to a clean saucepan and reheat until boiling. Set aside to cool slightly before serving warm.

garlic and lemon dressing

serves 4

2 tablespoons lemon juice

80 ml (2 1/2 fl oz/1/3 cup) oil

1 teaspoon wholegrain
mustard

1 garlic clove

freshly ground white pepper

Serve drizzled over a green salad.

1 Whisk the lemon juice, oil and mustard in a
   small bowl until combined. Add the garlic clove
   and set aside to infuse for 30 minutes.

2 Remove the garlic clove and whisk again before
   serving. Season with salt and white pepper.

Genovese pesto sauce

serves 4

Serve with pasta.

2 garlic cloves

50 g (1³/₄ oz) pine nuts

1 bunch (120 g/4¹/₂ oz) basil, stems removed

150–180 ml (5–6 fl oz) extra virgin olive oil

50 g (1³/₄ oz) Parmesan cheese, finely grated, plus extra to serve

1 Put the garlic and pine nuts in a mortar and pestle or food processor and pound or process until finely ground.

2 Add the basil and then drizzle in the olive oil a little at a time while pounding or processing. When you have a thick purée stop adding the oil.

3 Season and mix in the Parmesan.

ginger dipping sauce

serves 4-6

Serve with pieces of steamed or roast chicken or duck or with any Chinese-style starter.

55 g (2 oz/^{1}/$_3$ cup) grated fresh ginger

2 tablespoons peanut oil

2 tablespoons sweet chilli sauce

1 teaspoon caster (superfine) sugar

1 tablespoon chopped coriander (cilantro) leaves

1 Combine the ginger, peanut oil, sweet chilli sauce, sugar and coriander in a small bowl.

ginger and sesame dressing

serves 8

Serve over mixed Asian salad greens or steamed Asian greens.

1 teaspoon sesame oil

3 teaspoons rice wine vinegar

1 teaspoon finely grated orange zest

2 tablespoons orange juice

2 teaspoons grated fresh ginger

125 ml (4 fl oz/1/2 cup) vegetable oil

1 Combine the sesame oil, vinegar, orange zest, orange juice and ginger in a small bowl.

2 Gradually whisk in the vegetable oil until well blended. Season with salt and freshly ground black pepper.

gorgonzola and sage sauce

serves 4

Serve with pasta or gnocchi.

60 g butter

2 cloves garlic, crushed

1/2 cup (10 g) fresh small
sage leaves

100 g gorgonzola cheese

150 ml cream

1 cup (100 g) grated
Parmesan

1 Melt the butter in a small saucepan over medium heat, add the garlic and sage leaves and cook for a few minutes, or until the leaves start to crispen and the garlic browns a little. Pour the sage butter evenly over the cooked pasta or gnocchi.

2 Dot small knobs of the gorgonzola evenly among the pasta or gnocchi. Pour the cream over the top and sprinkle with the Parmesan.

3 Place under the grill and cook until the top starts to brown and the gnocchi or pasta is heated through.

gravy

serves 8

pan juices from roast beef,
lamb, chicken or pork

2 tablespoons plain
(all-purpose) flour

500 ml (17 fl oz/2 cups) beef
or chicken stock

Serve with roast beef, lamb, chicken or pork,
and roast potatoes or Yorkshire pudding.

1 Pour off any excess fat from the roasting tin.
Sprinkle the flour over the pan juices and stir
well, scraping any sediment from the bottom of
the roasting tin. Place the tin on the stove over
medium heat and cook, stirring, for 1–2minutes.

2 Add the stock a little at a time, stirring well.
Make sure the stock and the flour mixture are
well combined before adding more stock, or the
gravy will be lumpy. Bring to the boil and cook,
stirring, for 1 minute, or until the gravy has
thickened a little. Season to taste and serve
immediately with the roast.

Note: The gravy may be strained to remove any dark
flecks or meat particles.

green goddess dressing

serves 6-8

Serve as a salad dressing or with seafood.

375 g (13 oz/1 1/2 cups) whole-egg mayonnaise

4 anchovy fillets, mashed

4 spring onions (scallions), finely chopped

1 garlic clove, crushed

3 tablespoons chopped flat-leaf (Italian) parsley

3 tablespoons finely snipped chives

1 teaspoon tarragon vinegar

1   Combine the mayonnaise, anchovies, spring onions, garlic, parsley, chives and tarragon vinegar.

green chilli, mint and yoghurt sauce

serves 4

Serve with lamb.

1 large green chilli,
seeded and chopped

1 large handful mint

1 red Asian shallot, chopped

3 cm (1¹/4 inch) piece
ginger, chopped

2 teaspoons fish sauce

2 teaspoons lime juice

1 teaspoon shaved palm
sugar or soft brown sugar

250 g (9 oz/1 cup)
Greek-style yoghurt

1 To make the sauce, put the chilli, mint, shallot, ginger, fish sauce, lime juice and sugar in a small processor fitted with the metal blade. Whizz for 30 seconds, or until the mixture forms a rough paste.

2 Transfer to a small bowl and stir in the yoghurt. Cover and refrigerate until needed. Store the sauce, covered, in the refrigerator for up to 2 days.

green peppercorn sauce

serves 4

125 ml (4 fl oz/¹/₂ cup) chicken stock

pan juices from pan-fried steaks or chicken

125 ml (4 fl oz/¹/₂ cup) cream (whipping)

2 teaspoons tinned green peppercorns, rinsed and drained

2 teaspoons brandy

Serve with pan-fried steaks or boneless, skinless chicken breasts.

1 Pour the stock into the frying pan containing the pan juices. Stir over low heat until boiling, then add the cream and peppercorns. Boil, stirring constantly, for 2 minutes.

2 Add the brandy and boil for 1 minute more. Remove from the heat and serve immediately.

Rinse the peppercorns under running water and set aside.

Pan-fry the meat, then add the stock to the meat juices in the pan.

Boil until reduced slightly, then add the brandy and boil for another minute.

harissa dressing

serves 4-6

Serve with couscous.

80 ml (2^1/$_2$ fl oz/^{1}/$_3$ cup)
olive oil

2 tablespoons lime or
lemon juice

2 teaspoons harissa

1 small garlic clove, crushed

1   Whisk the olive oil, lime juice, harissa and garlic
    in a small bowl until combined.

herb mayonnaise

serves 4

125 g (4¹/2 oz/¹/2 cup)
whole-egg mayonnaise

1 tablespoon chopped parsley

1 tablespoon snipped chives

2 teaspoons chopped capers

Serve with fish patties or barbecued white fish fillets.

1 Combine the mayonnaise, parsley, chives and capers in a small bowl and mix well.

herb vinaigrette

serves 4

Serve drizzled over a green salad.

2 tablespoons white
wine vinegar

80 ml (2¹/₂ fl oz/¹/₃ cup)
light olive oil

1 tablespoon finely chopped
mixed herbs, such as
tarragon, dill, chives or basil

1 teaspoon Dijon mustard

freshly ground white pepper

1 Whisk the vinegar, olive oil, herbs and mustard
   in a small bowl until combined. Season with salt
   and white pepper and whisk until well blended.

herb vinegar

makes 1 litre (35 fl oz)

Use in place of white wine vinegar for a
flavoured vinaigrette.

1 litre (35 fl oz/4 cups) white
wine vinegar

3 tablespoons herbs, such as
tarragon, dill, chives or basil

herb sprig

1 Combine the white wine vinegar and herbs. Pour
   into a sterilized bottle and seal. Set aside for a
   week, shaking the bottle occasionally.

2 Strain the vinegar into a clean sterilized bottle
   and add a fresh herb sprig.

hollandaise sauce

175 g (6 oz) butter

4 egg yolks

1 tablespoon lemon juice

Serve with asparagus, egg dishes, poached salmon or chicken.

1 Melt the butter in a small saucepan. Skim any froth from the surface. Set the butter aside to cool.

2 Mix the egg yolks with 2 tablespoons of water in a small saucepan. Beat with a wire whisk for 30 seconds, or until the mixture is pale and foamy. Whisk over very low heat for 2–3 minutes, or until the mixture is thick and the whisk leaves a trail — do not let the pan get too hot or the egg yolks will scramble. Remove from the heat.

3 Add the cooled butter, a little at a time, whisking well after each addition. Try to avoid using the milky butter whey in the bottom of the pan. Stir in the lemon juice, season to taste and serve immediately.

Note: To prepare the hollandaise in a food processor, process the egg yolks, water and lemon juice for 10 seconds. With the motor running, add the cooled, melted butter in a thin stream.

lemon, lime and thyme vinegar

**makes 1 litre
(35 fl oz)**

Use in place of white wine vinegar for a
flavoured vinaigrette.

2 limes

4 lemons

1 litre (35 fl oz/4 cups) white
wine vinegar

20 thyme sprigs

1 Finely grate the zest of the limes and lemons.
Squeeze the juice from the lime and two of
the lemons.

2 Put the vinegar, lime juice, lemon juice, lime
zest, half the lemon zest and half the thyme
sprigs in a saucepan. Bring to the boil, then
reduce the heat and simmer for 5 minutes.
Remove from the heat and set aside at room
temperature until cold.

3 Meanwhile, put the remaining lemon zest into a
warm sterilized jar and add the remaining thyme
sprigs. Strain the vinegar and pour it into the jar.
Seal and store in a cool place for a week.

4 Line a funnel with muslin and strain the vinegar
into warm sterilized bottles. Seal and label. Store
for up to a year.

lemon grass and lime dressing

serves 10-12

Serve drizzled over mixed Asian salad greens.

125 ml (4 fl oz/1/2 cup)
vegetable oil

125 ml (4 fl oz/1/2 cup)
lime juice

3 teaspoons sesame oil

2 tablespoons thinly sliced
lemon grass, white part only

1 garlic clove, crushed

2 teaspoons soft brown sugar

1 Whisk the vegetable oil, lime juice, sesame oil, lemon grass, garlic and brown sugar in a bowl until combined. Season with salt and pepper and whisk to combine.

lemon sauce

serves 4

Serve with pan-fried boneless, skinless chicken breasts.

pan juices from pan-fried chicken

100 g (3½ oz) butter

2 tablespoons lemon juice

4 tablespoons shredded basil or parsley

1 Drain the excess fat from the pan containing the pan juices. Add the butter and cook over medium heat until the butter turns light brown.

2 Stir in the lemon juice and basil. Season lightly and serve immediately.

lemon thyme and lime dressing

serves 8

Serve drizzled over a green salad.

170 ml (5^1/$_2$ fl oz/^{2}/$_3$ cup)
light olive oil

80 ml (2^1/$_2$ fl oz/^{1}/$_3$ cup)
lime juice

2 tablespoons lemon thyme

1 teaspoon honey

1 Whisk the olive oil, lime juice, lemon thyme
   and honey in a bowl until combined. Season
   with salt and freshly ground black pepper and
   whisk well.

lentil sauce

serves 4

Serve with pasta.

1 litre chicken stock

1/3 cup (80 ml) virgin olive oil

1 onion, chopped

2 carrots, diced

3 celery sticks, diced

3 cloves garlic, crushed

1 tablespoon plus
1 teaspoon chopped
fresh thyme

400 g can lentils, drained

1 Boil the chicken stock in a large saucepan for 10 minutes, or until reduced to 2 cups (500 ml) of liquid.

2 Heat the oil in a large, deep frying pan, add the onion, carrot and celery and cook over medium heat for 10 minutes, or until browned.

3 Add two thirds of the crushed garlic and 1 tablespoon of the thyme and cook for a further minute. Add the stock, bring to the boil and cook for 8 minutes, or until reduced slightly and the vegetables are tender. Gently stir in the lentils until heated through.

4 Stir in the remaining garlic and thyme, and season with plenty of salt and black pepper— the stock should be slightly syrupy.

lime mayonnaise

serves 4-6

Serve with fried corn cakes or barbequed meats.

2 egg yolks

1 garlic clove, crushed

80 ml (2^1/$_2$ fl oz/^{1}/$_3$ cup) vegetable oil

80 ml (2^1/$_2$ fl oz/^{1}/$_3$ cup) olive oil

2 tablespoons lime juice

1 small green chilli, finely chopped

1 Put the egg yolks and garlic in a small bowl. Slowly add the vegetable oil, drop by drop, whisking continuously to form a smooth paste. When all the vegetable oil has been added, slowly add the olive oil in a thin stream while continuing to whisk.

2 Add the lime juice and chilli and mix well. Season to taste with salt and pepper.

lime and chilli raita

serves 4

3 handfuls mint, chopped

3 handfuls coriander
(cilantro) leaves, chopped

1 teaspoon grated lime zest

1 tablespoon lime juice

1 teaspoon grated fresh ginger

1 jalapeño chilli, seeded and
finely chopped (see note)

250 g (9 oz/1 cup) plain yoghurt

Serve with chicken, seafood, chargrilled tuna,
smoked or poached salmon, asparagus
or artichokes.

1 Combine the mint, coriander, lime zest, lime
juice, ginger and chilli in a bowl.

2 Fold the yoghurt through the lime mixture.
Season to taste with salt and freshly ground
black pepper.

Note: Jalapeño chillies are smooth and thick-
fleshed and are available both red and green.
They are quite fiery and you can use a less
powerful variety of chilli if you prefer.

It's a good idea to wear gloves to
de-seed chillies, to prevent skin
irritation.

Mix together the mint, coriander,
lime rind, juice, ginger and chilli.

Check the taste of the sauce before
seasoning with salt and black
pepper.

mandarin sauce

serves 8

310 g (11 oz) tin mandarin segments

2 tablespoons cornflour(cornstarch)

1 litre (35 fl oz/4 cups) chicken stock

125 ml (4 fl oz/$^1/_2$ cup) orange juice

2 tablespoons lemon juice

1 tablespoon honey

1 tablespoon soy sauce

2 teaspoons grated fresh ginger

1 tablespoon sugar

Serve with roast duck.

1 Process the undrained mandarin segments in a blender or food processor until smooth.

2 Put the cornflour in a small saucepan, add a little stock and stir until smooth. Add the remaining stock, orange juice, lemon juice, honey, soy sauce, ginger, sugar and mandarin purée. Stir over medium heat until the sauce boils and thickens. Serve hot.

mango salsa

serves 4-6

2 mangoes, chopped

3 spring onions (scallions), finely chopped

3 handfuls mint, chopped

1 tablespoon lime or lemon juice

Serve with chargrilled or barbecued meat, chicken or fish.

1 Combine the mango, spring onion, mint, lime juice and some freshly ground black pepper in a glass or ceramic bowl.

2 Cover with plastic wrap and set aside for at least 15 minutes before serving at room temperature.

marsala sauce

serves 4

Serve with pan-fried boneless, skinless chicken breasts, lamb or pork.

pan juices from pan-fried chicken

125 ml (4 fl oz/^{1}/2 cup) dry Marsala

125 ml (4 fl oz/^{1}/2 cup) chicken stock

80 ml (2^1/2 fl oz/^{1}/3 cup) cream (whipping)

1 Drain the excess fat from the frying pan containing the pan juices. Add the Marsala and cook over medium heat for 1–2 minutes, using a wooden spoon to scrape the sediment off the base of the pan.

2 Add the stock and cream. Bring to the boil, then reduce the heat and simmer for 5–6 minutes, or until thickened and reduced. Strain the sauce to remove any sediment. Serve immediately.

mango sauce

serves 4

Serve with peeled, cooked prawns (shrimp).

1 large mango, chopped

125 ml (4 fl oz/1/2 cup) coconut cream

1 tablespoon lime juice

2 teaspoons chopped mint

1 Process the mango, coconut cream and lime juice in a food processor until smooth.

2 Stir in the mint and season to taste with salt and freshly ground black pepper. Serve chilled.

mustard, honey and chive butter

makes a 20 cm (8 inch) log

Serve with hot steaks or fish.

250 g (9 oz) butter, softened

1 tablespoon honey

2 garlic cloves, roughly chopped

1 1/2 tablespoons snipped chives

1 1/2 tablespoons wholegrain mustard

1 1/2 teaspoons grated orange zest

1 Put the butter, honey and garlic in a small processor fitted with the plastic blade and whizz for 30 seconds, or until smooth and fluffy. Scrape down the side of the bowl as needed. Add the chives, mustard and orange zest and season with salt and freshly ground black pepper. Whizz just until combined.

2 Spoon the butter onto a sheet of plastic wrap, moulding it into a rough log shape. Gently guide the wrap around the butter to form a 20 cm (8 inch) cylinder. Twist the ends to tighten and wrap the log in a sheet of foil. Chill until ready to use.

3 To serve, cut 1 cm (1/2 inch) slices of butter and place on hot steaks or fish to melt, creating a sauce.

4 Store the butter in the refrigerator for up to 1 week. Alternatively, it can be frozen and sliced as needed.

mustard sauce

serves 4-6

250 ml (9 fl oz/1 cup)
chicken stock

6 spring onions (scallions),
finely chopped

1 tablespoon white
wine vinegar

2 tablespoons
wholegrain mustard

250 g (9 oz/1 cup) sour cream

Serve over pan-fried or grilled (broiled) pork, lamb or veal.

1 Combine the stock, spring onion, vinegar and mustard in a saucepan. Bring to the boil and cook for 5 minutes, or until the liquid has reduced by half.

2 Stir in the sour cream and heat through without boiling. Serve warm.

parsley béchamel

serves 4

Serve with fish or corned beef.

250 ml (9 fl oz/1 cup) milk
1 slice of onion
1 bay leaf
6 peppercorns
30 g (1 oz) butter
1 tablespoon plain (all-purpose) flour
3 tablespoons finely chopped parsley
freshly ground white pepper

1 Put the milk, onion, bay leaf and peppercorns in a small saucepan. Bring to the boil, then remove from the heat. Set aside to infuse for 10 minutes, then strain the milk.

2 Melt the butter in a small saucepan and add the flour. Cook, stirring, for 1 minute, or until the mixture is golden and bubbling. Remove from the heat and gradually add the infused milk, stirring after each addition until completely smooth. Return to the heat and stir until the mixture boils. Continue cooking for 1 minute, or until thick.

3 Remove from the heat and stir in the parsley. Season with salt and white pepper. Serve hot.

peach and basil vinegar

makes **425 ml (15 fl oz)**

430 g (15¹/₄ oz/2 cups) drained tinned peach slices

250 ml (9 fl oz/1 cup) white wine vinegar

2 large handfuls basil

Use in place of white wine vinegar for a flavoured vinaigrette.

1 Put the drained peach slices, vinegar and half the basil in a saucepan. Bring to the boil, then reduce the heat and simmer for 5 minutes. Remove from the heat and set aside at room temperature until cold.

2 Put the remaining basil in a warm sterilized jar. Remove the peach slices and basil from the vinegar and pour the liquid into the jar. Seal and set aside in a cool place for a week.

3 Line a funnel with muslin and strain the vinegar into warm sterilized bottles. Seal and label. Store for up to a year.

peach salsa

serves 4

3 tablespoons white wine vinegar

2 tablespoons caster (superfine) sugar

2 teaspoons grated fresh ginger

1 clove garlic, crushed

1/2 teaspoon ground cumin

1/4 cup (15 g/1/2 oz) chopped coriander (cilantro) leaves

1/4 cup (15 g/1/2 oz) chopped mint

1 red capsicum (pepper), sliced

1 small red onion, finely diced

1 small red chilli, finely chopped

3 canned or fresh peaches, diced

Serve with chargrilled or barbecued seafood or chicken.

1 Combine the vinegar, sugar, ginger, garlic, cumin, coriander and mint.

2 Put the capsicum, onion, chilli and peaches in a large bowl. Gently stir through the vinegar herb mixture and serve at once.

Use fresh peaches if they are in season, otherwise canned will suffice.

Mix together the vinegar, sugar, ginger, garlic, cumin, coriander and mint.

Stir through the vinegar herb mixture and serve at once.

peanut sauce

Serve with lamb kebabs.

1 onion, chopped

2 cloves garlic, crushed

2 teaspoons sambal oelek
or chilli paste

1 stem lemon grass,
white part only, chopped

2 teaspoons chopped
fresh ginger

1^{1}/$_{2}$ tablespoons oil

270 ml (9^{1}/$_{2}$ fl oz/1 cup)
coconut cream

^{1}/$_{2}$ cup (125 g) crunchy
peanut butter

1^{1}/$_{2}$ tablespoons fish sauce

2 teaspoons soy sauce

1 tablespoon grated palm
sugar or soft brown sugar

2 tablespoons lime juice

2 tablespoons chopped fresh
coriander leaves

1 Put the onion, garlic, sambal oelek, lemon grass and ginger in a food processor and process to a smooth paste.

2 Heat the oil in a saucepan over medium heat, add the paste and cook, stirring, for 2–3 minutes, or until fragrant. Add the coconut cream, peanut butter, fish sauce, soy sauce, sugar and lime juice and bring to the boil. Reduce the heat and simmer for 5 minutes, then stir in the coriander.

pesto

serves 6

50 g (1³/4 oz/¹/3 cup)
pine nuts

4 large handfuls basil

2 garlic cloves, crushed

35 g (1¹/4 oz/¹/3 cup) finely
grated Parmesan cheese

80 ml (2¹/2fl oz/¹/3 cup)
olive oil

Serve with pasta, grilled (broiled) fish, chicken or tomatoes. Pesto can also be used as a spread on crackers and is ideal for finger food.

1 Cook the pine nuts in a dry frying pan for 2–3 minutes, or until lightly browned. Transfer to a food processor and add the basil, garlic and Parmesan. Process until finely chopped.

2 With the motor running, add the olive oil in a thin stream. Season if necessary.

Toast the pine nuts in a dry frying pan until they are golden brown.

Put the basil, garlic, Parmesan and pine nuts in a food processor.

Add the olive oil in a thin stream with the motor running.

pink peppercorn sauce

serves 4

Serve with steaks.

60 g butter

1 tablespoon oil

1/2 cup (125 ml) white wine

2 tablespoons brandy

1/2 cup (125 ml) beef stock

2 tablespoons pink peppercorns in brine, drained and rinsed

1/2 cup (125 ml) cream

1 Heat the butter and oil in a large frying pan, add the wine and brandy and simmer for 4 minutes, or until reduced by half.

2 Add the beef stock and reduce by half again (you should have just over 1/2 cup/125 ml sauce). Meanwhile, roughly chop half the peppercorns.

3 Stir in all the peppercorns and the cream, and cook gently until the sauce has thickened slightly.

pistachio and lime sauce

serves 4

1 1/2 slices white bread, crusts removed

100 g (3 1/2 oz/2/3 cup) pistachio kernels

grated zest of 1 lime

1 garlic clove, chopped

50 g (1 3/4 oz/1/2 cup) grated Parmesan cheese

1 handful flat-leaf (Italian) parsley

2 teaspoons thyme

60 ml (2 fl oz/1/4 cup) olive oil

250 ml (9 fl oz/1 cup) of hot water.

Serve with pasta.

1 Put the bread in a mini processor and whizz for 30 seconds, or until breadcrumbs form.

2 Add the pistachios, lime zest, garlic, Parmesan, parsley and thyme to the processor containing the crumbs and whizz for 25 seconds, or until the mixture forms a coarse paste. With the motor running, gradually add the olive oil. Season well with salt and freshly ground black pepper.

3 Add enough of the water to make a coating consistency. Serve immediately.

plum sauce

serves 4

Serve with pork or deep-fried crumbed calamari.

1 teaspoon oil

1 garlic clove, crushed

310 g (11 oz/1 cup) dark plum jam

80 ml (2½ fl oz/⅓ cup) white vinegar

1–2 tablespoons bottled chopped chilli or sweet chilli sauce

1 Heat the oil in a small saucepan. Add the garlic and cook until just starting to turn golden.

2 Add the jam, vinegar and chilli and stir over medium heat until well blended. Thin with a little warm water if necessary. Serve warm or at room temperature.

ponzu sauce

serves 6-8

Serve with sashimi.

1½ tablespoons
rice vinegar

150 ml (5 fl oz) soy sauce

60 ml (2 fl oz/¼ cup)
strained lemon juice

1 tablespoon mirin

100 ml (3½ fl oz) dashi
(see note)

1 Combine the vinegar, soy sauce, lemon juice, mirin and dashi. Cover and refrigerate overnight before serving.

NOTE: To make the dashi, dissolve ¼ teaspoon of instant dashi granules in 125 ml (4 fl oz/½ cup) of boiling water and stir until dissolved.

prune and cointreau sauce

serves 8

Serve with roast pork.

250 g (9 oz/1 cup)
pitted prunes

250 ml (9 fl oz/1 cup)
white wine

185 ml (6 fl oz/3/4 cup)
orange juice

2 tablespoons Cointreau or
other orange liqueur

20 g (3/4 oz) butter, chilled
and cubed

1 Put the prunes, wine, 125 ml (4 fl oz/1/2 cup) of the orange juice, half the liqueur and 60 ml (2 fl oz/1/4 cup) of water in a saucepan. Bring to the boil, then reduce the heat and simmer for 10 minutes.

2 Remove from the heat and add the remaining orange juice and liqueur and 60 ml (2 fl oz/1/4 cup) of water. Set aside to cool slightly.

3 Pass the sauce through a fine sieve into a clean saucepan. Heat before serving and whisk in the cubed butter, a few pieces at a time. The sauce will thicken slightly as the butter is added. Serve warm.

quick satay sauce

250 ml (9 fl oz/1 cup) pineapple juice

250 g (9 oz/1 cup) peanut butter

1/2 teaspoon garlic powder

1/2 teaspoon onion powder

2 tablespoons sweet chilli sauce

60 ml (2 fl oz/1/4 cup) soy sauce

Serve with grilled (broiled) or barbecued beef or chicken kebabs.

1 Combine the pineapple juice, peanut butter, garlic powder, onion powder, sweet chilli sauce and soy sauce in a small saucepan. Stir over medium heat until the mixture is smooth and heated through.

2 Add a little water for a thinner sauce, if preferred. Reheat in a saucepan over medium heat before serving.

ranch dressing

125 g (41/2 oz/1/2 cup) whole-egg mayonnaise

125 g (41/2 oz/1/2 cup) sour cream

2 tablespoons lemon juice

2 tablespoons snipped chives

freshly ground white pepper

Serve with chicken wings.

1 Combine the mayonnaise, sour cream, lemon juice and chives in a bowl. Season with salt and white pepper and mix well.

raspberry vinaigrette

serves 4

80 ml (2^1/$_2$ fl oz/^{1}/$_3$ cup)
hazelnut oil

2 tablespoons
raspberry vinegar

5 raspberries, finely chopped

^{1}/$_2$ teaspoon sugar

freshly ground white pepper

Serve drizzled over a green salad.

1 Whisk the hazelnut oil, vinegar, raspberries and sugar in a small bowl. Season with salt and white pepper and whisk to combine.

raspberry vinegar

makes 500 ml (17 fl oz)

290 g (10¹/4 oz/2¹/3 cups)
raspberries

500 ml (17 fl oz/2 cups)
white wine vinegar

2 teaspoons caster
(superfine) sugar

2–3 raspberries,
extra, optional

Use in place of white wine vinegar for a flavoured vinaigrette.

1 Place the raspberries in a non-metallic bowl and crush gently with the back of a spoon.

2 Warm the vinegar in a saucepan over low heat. Add the vinegar to the raspberries and mix well. Pour the mixture into a sterilized glass bottle and set aside in a warm place for two weeks, shaking regularly.

3 Strain the vinegar through a muslin-lined sieve into a small saucepan. Add the sugar and stir over medium heat until the sugar has dissolved. Pour into the clean, warm, sterilized bottle. Add the extra raspberries, if using. Seal and label the bottle and store in a cool, dark place for up to 12 months.

red curry sauce with mushrooms

Serve with steamed rice.

500 ml (2 cups) coconut cream

2 teaspoons red curry paste

2 teaspoons finely chopped lemon grass, white part only

125 ml (1/2 cup) vegetable stock

250 ml (1 cup) coconut milk

2 teaspoons mushroom soy sauce

1 1/2 tablespoons shaved palm sugar

3 fresh makrut (kaffir) lime leaves

1 tablespoon lime juice

400 g (14 oz) assorted mushrooms (shiitake, oyster, enoki, button)

2 tablespoons coriander (cilantro) leaves

3 tablespoons torn Thai basil

1 Place the coconut cream in a wok, bring to the boil and cook over high heat for 2–3 minutes. Add the curry paste and chopped lemon grass and cook, stirring continuously, for 3–4 minutes, or until fragrant.

2 Reduce the heat to medium, add the stock, coconut milk, soy sauce, palm sugar, lime leaves and lime juice. Cook, stirring, for 3–4 minutes, or until the sugar has dissolved. Stir in the assorted mushrooms and cook for 3–4 minutes, or until tender.

3 Remove from the heat, stir in the coriander and basil and serve with steamed rice.

red wine gravy

serves 6

Serve with roast beef.

pan juices from roast beef

2 tablespoons plain
(all-purpose) flour

80 ml (2¹/₂ fl oz/¹/₃ cup)
red wine

625 ml (21¹/₂ fl oz/2¹/₂
cups) beef stock

1 Drain off all but 2 tablespoons of the pan juices
from the roasting tin. Place the tin on the stove
over low heat. Sprinkle the flour over the pan
juices and stir well, scraping any sediment from
the bottom of the tin. Cook over medium heat,
stirring constantly, for 1–2 minutes, or until the
flour is well browned.

2 Combine the red wine and stock and gradually
stir into the flour mixture, making sure the liquid
is well incorporated after each addition. Heat,
stirring constantly, until the gravy boils and
thickens. Reduce the heat and simmer for
3 minutes, then season to taste with salt and
freshly ground black pepper. Serve warm.

red wine sauce

serves 4

Serve over pan-fried beef steaks or lamb cutlets.

30 g (1 oz) butter

pan juices from pan-fried
beef steaks or
lamb cutlets

1 small onion, thinly sliced

1 teaspoon plain
(all-purpose) flour

2 teaspoons soft
brown sugar

185 ml (6 fl oz/3/4 cup)
red wine

1 Melt the butter in the frying pan containing the pan juices over medium heat. Add the onion and cook, stirring, for 5 minutes, or until the onion is very soft. Add the flour and sugar and cook for 1 minute.

2 Gradually add the red wine, stirring constantly. Bring to the boil, then reduce the heat and simmer, stirring, for 5 minutes, or until the sauce has reduced by half. Season with salt and freshly ground black pepper. Serve warm.

roasted cashew satay sauce

serves 10

Serve with chicken or pork kebabs, barbecued meats or sausa

250 g (9 oz/1²/3 cups) roasted cashew nuts

150 g (5¹/2 oz/1 cup) roasted peanuts

1 teaspoon cumin seeds

1 teaspoon coriander seeds

1/4 teaspoon fenugreek seeds

375 ml (13 fl oz/1¹/4 cups) coconut milk

3 teaspoons kecap manis or thick soy sauce

2 teaspoons sweet chilli sauce

1 teaspoon soft brown sugar

1 Preheat the oven to 160°C (315°F/Gas 2–3). Roast the nuts on a baking tray for 10 minutes, then set aside to cool.

2 Finely grind the cumin, coriander and fenugreek seeds with a mortar and pestle. Fry over low heat in a dry frying pan, shaking the pan regularly, for 3 minutes, or until aromatic.

3 Finely chop the nuts and spices in a food processor. Add the coconut milk, kecap manis or soy sauce, sweet chilli sauce and sugar and season to taste.

4 Transfer the sauce to a saucepan and gently heat through. Serve warm.

roasted corn and avocado salsa

serves 6

2 corn cobs, husks removed

1 avocado, chopped

85 g (3 oz/$^1/_2$ cup) stuffed green olives, chopped

2 tablespoons finely chopped parsley

3 spring onions (scallions), shredded

1 tablespoon olive oil

2 tablespoons lemon juice

Serve with pan-fried salmon, chicken, lamb or beef.

1 Cook the corn in a saucepan of boiling water for 5 minutes, or until just soft. Drain, cool and pat dry with paper towels. Using a large sharp knife, cut the kernels from the cobs and place in a single layer on a foil-lined tray. Cook under a very hot grill (broiler) for 10 minutes, or until golden brown, turning once to ensure even roasting. Set aside to cool.

2 Combine the corn, avocado, olives, parsley, spring onion, olive oil and lemon juice. Season liberally with salt and freshly ground black pepper. Toss well to make sure the avocado is coated with the dressing. Cover and refrigerate for 15 minutes before serving.

roasted pumpkin sauce

serves 4-6

500 g (1 lb 2 oz)
pumpkin (squash)

2 tablespoons olive oil

2 garlic cloves, crushed

2 teaspoons cumin seeds

2 teaspoons coriander seeds

250 ml (9 fl oz/1 cup)
vegetable stock

Serve with pasta, a vegetarian nut roast or roast beef.

1 Preheat the oven to 200°C (400°F/Gas 6). Cut the pumpkin into wedges, leaving the skin on, and place in a roasting tin. Combine the olive oil and garlic and drizzle over the pumpkin. Season with salt and pepper. Roast for 1 hour, or until the pumpkin is tender. Set aside to cool slightly.

2 Fry the cumin seeds and coriander seeds in a dry frying pan for 5 minutes. Transfer to a food processor or mortar and pestle and process until ground.

3 Remove the skin from the pumpkin. Purée the pumpkin flesh, ground spices and stock in a food processor until smooth. Transfer to a saucepan and gently heat through.

roasted red capsicum salsa

serves 6

Serve with chargrilled lamb steaks, veal, beef, chicken, fish or seafood.

2 red capsicums (peppers), seeded and quartered

2 tomatoes

1/2 small red onion, finely chopped

1–2 small red chillies, finely chopped

2 limes, peeled and segmented

2 tablespoons olive oil

1 teaspoon sugar

1   Preheat the oven to 180°C (350°F/Gas 4). Roast the capsicum in an oiled roasting tin for 30 minutes, turning regularly. If it begins to burn, add 2 tablespoons of water to the tin. Set aside to cool, then cut into small cubes.

2   Score a cross in the base of each tomato. Place the tomatoes in a heatproof bowl and cover with boiling water. Set aside for 30 seconds, then transfer to cold water and peel the skin away from the cross. Cut the tomatoes in half, scoop out the seeds and cut the flesh into thin strips.

3   Combine the capsicum, tomatoes, onion, chilli, lime segments, oil and sugar. Season with salt and freshly ground black pepper. Cover and set aside for at least 15 minutes before serving.

rocket salsa verde

serves 4

25 g (1 oz/½ cup)
fresh breadcrumbs

125 ml (4 fl oz/½ cup) olive
oil

2 tablespoons lemon juice

1 garlic clove, crushed

4 anchovy fillets,
finely chopped

30 g (1 oz/¾ cup) rocket
(arugula) leaves, chopped

1 small handful flat-leaf
(Italian) parsley, chopped

1 tablespoon capers, rinsed,
squeezed dry
and chopped

Serve with pan-fried fish, meat or chicken. Also good as a pasta sauce.

1 Combine the breadcrumbs, olive oil, lemon juice, garlic, anchovies, rocket, parsley and capers in a bowl. Season well with freshly ground black pepper.

2 Cover with plastic wrap and set aside at room temperature for 4 hours. Stir well just before serving.

It's a good idea to rinse the capers before using to wash off the brine.

Remove any tough stems from the rocket before chopping the leaves.

Mix together all the ingredients in a large bowl then leave at room temperature.

roasted red capsicum sauce

serves 8

2 red capsicums (peppers), seeded and quartered

2 tablespoons olive oil

1 red onion, roughly chopped

1–2 garlic cloves, crushed

425 g (15 oz) tin chopped tomatoes

3 handfuls chopped parsley

1 large handful chopped basil

1 tablespoon tomato paste (concentrated purée)

1 tablespoon caster (superfine) sugar

Serve with any grilled (broiled) meats or vegetables.

1 Cook the capsicum, skin side up, under a hot grill (broiler) for 10 minutes, or until blackened. Cool in a plastic bag for 10 minutes, then peel away the skin and chop the flesh.

2 Heat the oil in a saucepan and cook the onion and garlic for 2 minutes, or until soft but not brown. Add the tomatoes, parsley, basil, tomato paste, sugar and 375 ml (13 fl oz/1½ cups) of water.

3 Add the capsicum and cook, stirring often, over very low heat for 45 minutes–1 hour, or until thick. Cool slightly, then purée in batches in a food processor. Season to taste. Serve warm.

Once the skin is blackened it should peel away easily.

Cook the onion and garlic until they are softened but not browned.

Add the chopped capsicum to the sauce and cook for up to 1 hour, or until thick.

roasted walnut sauce

serves 8-10

300 g (10¹/₂ oz/2¹/₂ cups)
walnut pieces

1 tablespoon extra virgin
olive oil

¹/₄ teaspoon paprika

2 slices white bread,
crusts removed

300 ml (10¹/₂ fl oz) milk

1 garlic clove, crushed

4 tablespoons roughly
chopped parsley

125 ml (4 fl oz/¹/₂ cup) light
olive oil

25 g (1 oz/¹/₄ cup) grated
Parmesan cheese

Serve with chargrilled vegetables or pasta.

1 Preheat the oven to 190°C (375°F/Gas 5). Put the walnuts on a baking tray and toss with the extra virgin olive oil. Sprinkle with the paprika and a pinch of salt and toss well. Roast for 5 minutes, then set aside to cool.

2 Soak the bread in the milk until soft.

3 Process the walnuts, bread and milk mixture, garlic and parsley in a food processor until very fine.

4 With the motor running, slowly pour in the olive oil until the sauce is thick. Add the Parmesan, season to taste and process briefly to combine.

rocket pesto

serves 4-6

300 g (10^1/2 oz/2 bunches) rocket (arugula)

1–2 garlic cloves, crushed

80 g (2^3/4 oz/^{1}/2 cup) roasted macadamia nuts

50 g (1^3/4 oz/^{1}/2 cup) finely grated Parmesan cheese

125 ml (4 fl oz/^{1}/2 cup) extra virgin olive oil

Serve with pasta, grilled (broiled) fish or chicken.

1 Put the rocket leaves in a food processor. Add the garlic, macadamia nuts and Parmesan cheese and process until finely chopped.

2 With the motor running, add the olive oil in a thin stream until the pesto is thick and creamy. Season to taste.

romesco sauce

serves 6-8

4 garlic cloves, unpeeled

1 Roma (plum) tomato, halved and seeded

2 long red chillies

2 tablespoons blanched almonds

2 tablespoons hazelnuts

60 g (2¼ oz/⅓ cup) sun-dried capsicums (peppers) in oil, drained and chopped

1 tablespoon olive oil

1 tablespoon red wine vinegar

Serve with grilled (broiled) fish.

1   Preheat the oven to 200°C (400°F/Gas 6). Wrap the garlic in foil, put on a baking tray with the tomato and chillies and roast for 12 minutes. Spread the nuts on the tray and bake for 3–5 minutes. Set aside to cool for 15 minutes.

2   Blend the nuts in a blender until finely ground. Squeeze the garlic and scrape the tomato flesh into the blender, discarding the skins. Scrape the chilli flesh into the blender, discarding the seeds and skins. Add the capsicums, olive oil, vinegar, some salt and 2 tablespoons of water. Blend until smooth, adding more water, if necessary, to form a soft dipping consistency. Set aside for 30 minutes.

saffron dressing

serves 4

Serve with grilled seafood

pinch saffron threads

60 g (1/4 cup) mayonnaise

1 1/2 tablespoons cream

1 teaspoon lemon juice

1 Place the saffron threads in a bowl and soak in 2 teaspoons of hot water for 10 minutes.

2 Add the mayonnaise, mixing well, until it is a rich yellow in colour. Stir in the cream, then the lemon juice. Refrigerate until needed.

salsa verde

serves 4

3 handfuls flat-leaf
(Italian) parsley

4 tablespoons mint

3 tablespoons dill

2 tablespoons snipped chives

1 garlic clove, crushed

1 tablespoon lemon juice

5 anchovy fillets

35 g (1^1/4 oz/^{1}/4 cup) capers,
rinsed and squeezed dry

125 ml (4 fl oz/^{1}/2 cup)
olive oil

Serve with roast meats or grilled (broiled) fish
kebabs or prawns (shrimp).

1 Process the parsley, mint, dill, chives and garlic in
   a food processor for 30 seconds, or
   until combined.

2 Add the lemon juice, anchovies and capers and
   process until combined.

3 With the motor running, slowly add the olive oil
   in a thin stream and process until the mixture
   is smooth.

sambal oelek

serves 6-8

Serve with rice and curries.

200 g (7 oz/2¹/₂ cups) small
red chillies
1 teaspoon salt
1 teaspoon sugar
1 tablespoon vinegar
1 tablespoon oil

1   Remove the stalks from the chillies. Put the chillies
in a small saucepan with 250 ml (9 fl oz/1 cup) of
water and bring to the boil. Reduce the heat and
simmer, partially covered, for 15 minutes, then
set aside to cool slightly.

2   Transfer the chilli mixture to a food processor
and add the salt, sugar, vinegar and oil. Process
until the mixture is finely chopped. Set aside to
cool, then refrigerate in a sealed container for up
to two weeks.

satay sauce

serves 8

165 g (5³/4 oz/1 cup)
roasted unsalted peanuts

2 tablespoons olive oil

1 onion, chopped

2 garlic cloves, crushed

3 cm (1¹/4 inch) piece ginger,
grated

¹/2 teaspoon chilli powder

2 teaspoons curry powder

1 teaspoon ground cumin

400 ml (14 fl oz)
coconut milk

50 g (1³/4 oz/¹/4 cup) soft
brown sugar

1 tablespoon lemon juice

Serve with beef or chicken kebabs or with
grilled (broiled) chicken.

1 Process the peanuts in a food processor until
   finely chopped.

2 Heat the oil in a saucepan over medium heat
   and cook the onion for 5 minutes, or until
   softened. Add the garlic, ginger, chilli, curry and
   cumin and cook, stirring, for 2 minutes.

3 Add the coconut milk, brown sugar and peanuts.
   Reduce the heat and cook for 5 minutes, or until
   thickened. Add the lemon juice and season with
   salt. For a smooth sauce, process in a food
   processor for 30 seconds. Serve warm.

skordalia

serves 6

2 large floury potatoes
(500 g/1 lb 2 oz),
peeled and chopped

5 garlic cloves, crushed

55 g (2 oz/1/2 cup)
ground almonds

170 ml (51/2 fl oz/2/3 cup)
olive oil

2 tablespoons white
wine vinegar

Serve with steamed beetroot and beetroot greens, fish croquettes, seafood, steaks, lamb or chicken.

1 Boil the potatoes until tender; drain, then mash. Mash the garlic and almonds into the potato.

2 Gradually add the olive oil, mashing until smooth. Add the vinegar and season to taste. Mash well, adding 1 tablespoon of water at a time (you will need 3–4 tablespoons) to give a thick creamy consistency. Cover and refrigerate for up to a day. Serve cold.

smoky tomato sauce

makes about 1 litre

smoking mix

2 tablespoons Chinese or
Ceylon tea leaves

2 star anise, crushed

1 strip orange zest

1/2 teaspoon five-spice powder

6 juniper berries, crushed

sauce

2 onions, quartered

2 red capsicums (peppers),
cut into large pieces

2 red chillies, cut in half

3 tablespoons oil

3 garlic cloves, chopped

500 g (1 lb 2 oz) tomatoes, chopped

2 tablespoons Worcestershire sauce

125 ml (1/2 cup) ready-made
barbecue sauce

2 tablespoons
tamarind concentrate

1 tablespoon white vinegar

1 tablespoon soft brown sugar

Serve with barbecued meats.

1   Combine all the ingredients for the smoking mix in a bowl. Pour the mix into the centre of a sheet of foil and fold the edges to prevent spreading. (This will form an open container to allow the mix to smoke.) Place the foil container on the bottom of a dry wok or wide frying pan. Put an open rack or steamer in the wok or frying pan, making sure it is elevated over the mix.

2   Place the onion, capsicum and chilli on the rack and cover with a lid, or alternatively cover the entire wok or frying pan tightly with foil to prevent the smoke from escaping. Smoke over medium heat for about 10–15 minutes, or until the vegetables are tender. For a very smoky sauce cook the vegetables for longer; if you prefer it less so, reduce the time. Remove the smoking mix container.

3   Dice the onion, capsicum and chilli quite finely. Heat the oil in the wok and add the garlic and cooked vegetables. Fry over medium heat for 3 minutes, then add the tomato and cook until pulpy. Add the sauces, tamarind, vinegar and sugar. Simmer, stirring occasionally, for about 20–25 minutes, or until the sauce is quite thick. Store in the refrigerator.

soubise (onion sauce)

Serve with cooked meats.

50 g (1³/₄ oz) butter

1 large onion (200 g/7 oz), very finely chopped

250 ml (9 fl oz/1 cup) milk

1 onion, sliced, extra

3 peppercorns

1 bay leaf

1 tablespoon plain (all-purpose) flour

60 ml (2 fl oz/¹/₄ cup) cream (whipping)

1 Heat 30 g (1 oz) of the butter in a frying pan. Add the finely chopped onion and cook over low–medium heat until soft and translucent but not brown.

2 Put the milk, sliced onion, peppercorns and bay leaf in a small saucepan. Bring to the boil, then remove from the heat and set aside to infuse.

3 Melt the remaining butter in a saucepan over low heat. Stir in the flour and cook for 1 minute, or until foaming. Remove from the heat and strain in the milk, whisking thoroughly. Return to the heat and bring to the boil, whisking until thick. Season to taste. Reduce the heat and simmer for 2 minutes. Stir in the chopped onion and cream. Serve warm.

sour cherry sauce

serves 6

680 g (1 lb 8 oz) jar pitted morello (sour) cherries

80 ml (2½ fl oz/⅓ cup) port

1 teaspoon Dijon mustard

½ teaspoon grated orange zest

60 ml (2 fl oz/¼ cup) strained orange juice

1 chicken stock cube

1 tablespoon cornflour (cornstarch)

Serve with roast duck, turkey, pork, ham, smoked chicken or any type of poultry or game.

1 Drain the cherries, reserving 250 ml (9 fl oz/1 cup) of the liquid. Place the liquid in a saucepan with the port, mustard, orange zest and orange juice. Crumble in the stock cube and bring to the boil.

2 Blend the cornflour with 2 tablespoons of water and stir into the sauce. Bring to the boil and add the drained cherries, then reduce the heat and simmer, stirring occasionally, for 5 minutes. Season to taste and serve hot.

Drain the jar of morello cherries, reserving a cup of the liquid.

Crumble the stock cube into the liquid and then bring to the boil.

Dissolve the cornflour in a little water before adding, or it will form lumps.

soy and sesame dipping sauce

serves 8

Serve with Thai or Chinese starters. Also good with fried or steamed chicken or fish.

250 ml (9 fl oz/1 cup) rice vinegar or white wine vinegar

115 g (4 oz/^{1}/2 cup) caster (superfine) sugar

2 tablespoons dark soy sauce

^{1}/4 teaspoon salt

1 tablespoon sesame seeds, roasted

1 tablespoon honey

1 Combine the vinegar and sugar in a small saucepan. Stir over low heat until the sugar has dissolved.

2 Transfer the sugar mixture to a serving bowl and add the soy sauce, salt, sesame seeds and honey. Serve warm.

spanish tapas

**makes 250 ml
(9 fl oz/1 cup)**

80 ml (2¹/2 fl oz/¹/3 cup)
orange juice

pinch of saffron threads

125 ml (4 fl oz/¹/2 cup) extra
virgin olive oil

2 tablespoons lemon juice

2 garlic cloves, finely
chopped

1 bird's eye chilli, finely
chopped

3 tablespoons chopped dill

sea salt, to taste

Serve this dressing sparingly over warm
vegetables or chargrilled meats and seafood.

1 Put the orange juice and saffron in a small
saucepan and gently warm over low heat.
Remove from the heat and set aside for 5
minutes.

2 Put the oil, lemon juice, garlic and chilli in a
blender or small processor fitted with the metal
blade and whizz for 30 seconds, or until well
combined. Add the dill and the orange juice and
saffron mixture and whizz for 30 seconds.
Season with sea salt and freshly ground black
pepper, to taste. Store the dressing in an airtight
container in the refrigerator for 5–7 days.

spiced coconut sauce

serves 2-4

Serve with baked whole fish or chicken.

40 g (1¹/2 oz/¹/2 small bunch) coriander (cilantro)

2 teaspoons oil

3 cm (1¹/4 inch) piece ginger, grated

2 lemon grass stems, white part only, finely chopped

2 small red chillies, finely chopped

1 garlic clove, finely chopped

60–100 ml (2–3¹/2 fl oz) coconut cream

2 tablespoons rice vinegar

1 teaspoon soft brown sugar

1 Finely chop the coriander, keeping the roots, stems and leaves separate. Heat the oil in a frying pan over low heat and cook the coriander roots, ginger, lemon grass, chilli and garlic, stirring constantly, for 3 minutes, or until aromatic.

2 Stir in 60 ml (2 fl oz/¹/4 cup) of the coconut cream. Increase the heat to high and bring the sauce to a rapid boil. Cook for about 1 minute, or until the mixture looks oily. Add the remaining coconut cream if the sauce becomes too thick.

3 Transfer the mixture to a bowl and stir in the coriander stems and leaves, vinegar and brown sugar. Add salt and more sugar, to taste. Serve at room temperature.

Chop the bunch of coriander, keeping the root separate from the leaves and stem.

Cook the ginger, lemon grass, chilli, garlic and coriander root until aromatic.

Transfer to a bowl and add the coriander, rice vinegar and sugar.

strawberry vinaigrette

serves 6

Serve drizzled over a green salad.

80 ml (2^1/$_2$ fl oz/^{1}/$_3$ cup) light olive oil

2 tablespoons strawberry vinegar

^{1}/$_2$ teaspoon Dijon mustard

^{1}/$_2$ teaspoon sugar

1 Place all ingredients in a screw-topped jar and shake well. Will keep, covered, in the fridge for up to two days.

spicy chilli dipping sauce

serves 4

Serve with grilled or roasted meats.

2 lemon grass stems, white part only, chopped

8 coriander (cilantro) roots including 10 cm (4 inches) stems, chopped

7 cm (2³/4 inch) piece galangal, chopped

1 large red Asian shallot, chopped

2 garlic cloves, chopped

1 large green chilli, seeded and chopped

3 large tomatoes

1 tablespoon oil

60 ml (2 fl oz/¹/4 cup) fish sauce

25 g (1 oz/¹/4 cup) shaved palm sugar or soft brown sugar

2 teaspoons tamarind concentrate

2 tablespoons chopped coriander (cilantro) leaves

1 Put the lemon grass, coriander roots and stems, galangal, shallot, garlic and chilli in a small processorfitted with the metal blade. Whizz in 3–4 second bursts for 30 seconds, or until finely chopped.

2 Score a cross in the base of each tomato. Put in a heatproof bowl and cover with boiling water. Leave for 30 seconds, then transfer to cold water and peel the skin away from the cross. Roughly chop the tomatoes.

3 Heat the oil in a large heavy-based saucepan. Add the lemon grass paste, stir, then add two-thirds of the chopped tomato. Cook, stirring, for 5 minutes. Set aside to cool slightly, then transfer to the processor and whizz for 15 seconds, or until smooth. Add the remaining tomato and whizz in short bursts for 15 seconds, or until the mixture is finely chopped but still has texture.

4 Return the mixture to the saucepan and add the fish sauce, sugar and tamarind concentrate. Simmer, stirring frequently, for 10 minutes. Stir in the coriander leaves. Serve warm.

sweet chilli dressing

serves 4-6

1 red chilli, finely chopped

60 ml (2 fl oz/¹/4 cup) lemon juice

2 tablespoons soft brown sugar

2 tablespoons finely chopped coriander (cilantro) leaves

1 tablespoon fish sauce

1 tablespoon sweet chilli sauce

Serve drizzled over chargrilled baby octopus or use as a dip.

1 Whisk the chilli, lemon juice, brown sugar, coriander, fish sauce and sweet chilli sauce in a small bowl until well combined.

sweet chilli sauce

Serve with Thai starters such as spring rolls and fish cakes.

125 ml (4 fl oz/1/2 cup) white wine vinegar

165 g (5³/4 oz/³/4 cup) sugar

4 red chillies, roughly chopped

1 Put the vinegar, sugar, chilli and a pinch of salt in a small saucepan. Heat, stirring, without boiling, until the sugar has completely dissolved. Bring to the boil, then reduce the heat and simmer for 10 minutes. Set aside to cool.

2 Transfer the cooled chilli mixture to a food processor and process until the chilli is finely chopped.

tahini dressing

serves 4-6

2 tablespoons tahini

3 teaspoons lemon juice

1 small garlic clove, crushed

2 tablespoons sour cream

1 tablespoon chopped parsley

Serve with lamb koftas or barbecued lamb or drizzle over noodles.

1 Put the tahini, lemon juice, garlic, sour cream, parsley and a pinch of salt in a small bowl and stir to combine. Add 2–3 tablespoons of water and stir until creamy.

tamarind sauce

serves 4

Serve with crab or other crustaceans.

60 ml (¼ cup) sweet
chilli sauce

1 tablespoon Thai fish sauce

2 tablespoons soy sauce

2 tablespoons tamarind
purée or lemon juice

25 g (1 oz) grated palm
sugar or soft brown sugar

250 ml (1 cup) coconut milk

1 tablespoon water

1 tablespoon oil

2 large garlic cloves, crushed

2 small red chillies, seeded
and finely chopped

1 Mix together all the ingredients except the oil,
   garlic cloves and chilli in a jug.

2 Add the oil to the wok and, when hot, add the
   garlic and chillies. Cook for a minute, stirring,
   then add the sauce mixture. Bring to the boil,
   then reduce the heat to medium and leave to
   bubble away, without a lid, for 8–10 minutes, or
   until you have a thick sauce.

tartare sauce

serves 8

375 g (13 oz/1^1/2 cups) whole-egg mayonnaise

1 tablespoon finely chopped onion

1 teaspoon lemon juice

1 tablespoon chopped gherkins (pickles)

1 teaspoon chopped capers

^{1}/4 teaspoon Dijon mustard

1 tablespoon finely chopped parsley

Serve with deep-fried battered or crumbed fish or calamari rings.

1 Put the mayonnaise, onion, lemon juice, gherkins, capers, mustard and parsley in a bowl. Mix well and season with salt and pepper.

thousand island dressing

serves 6

Serve drizzled over a green salad.

125 g (4$^{1}/_{2}$ oz/$^{1}/_{2}$ cup) whole-egg mayonnaise

1 tablespoon tomato paste (concentrated purée)

1 teaspoon Dijon mustard

2 teaspoons malt vinegar

freshly ground white pepper

1 Put the mayonnaise, tomato paste, mustard and vinegar in a small bowl. Stir until well combined. Season to taste with salt and white pepper.

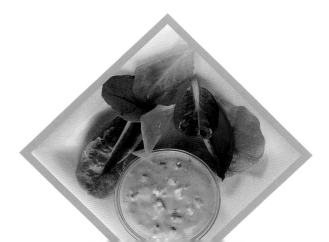

tomato and bacon sauce

serves 4

Serve with pasta.

1 tablespoon olive oil

170 g streaky bacon, thinly sliced

500 g Roma tomatoes, roughly chopped

$1/2$ cup (125 ml) thick cream

2 tablespoons sun-dried tomato pesto

2 tablespoons finely chopped fresh flat-leaf parsley

1 Heat the oil in a frying pan, add the bacon and cook over high heat for 2 minutes, or until starting to brown.

2 Reduce the heat to medium, add the tomato and cook, stirring frequently, for 2 minutes, or until the tomato has softened but still holds its shape.

3 Add the cream and tomato pesto and stir until heated through. Remove from the heat, add the parsley.

tomato and basil sauce

serves 4

Serve with pasta.

5 tablespoons extra virgin olive oil

5 cloves garlic, thinly sliced

6 vine-ripened tomatoes, seeded and chopped

3/4 cup (25 g) torn fresh basil leaves

1 Heat 4 tablespoons of the oil in a frying pan and cook the garlic over low heat for 1 minute.

2 As soon as the garlic begins to change colour, remove the pan from the heat and add the remaining oil, tomatoes and basil. Season generously with salt and ground black pepper.

tomato salsa

4 Roma (plum) tomatoes

1 red onion, finely chopped

1 bird's eye chilli, seeded and thinly sliced

3 tablespoons chopped coriander (cilantro) leaves

1–2 tablespoons lime juice

1/2 teaspoon salt

Serve with chicken, seafood, grilled (broiled) meats or Mexican food.

1 Cut the tomatoes in half horizontally and scoop out the seeds. Finely chop the tomato flesh and place it in a bowl.

2 Add the onion, chilli, coriander, lime juice and salt to the tomato and toss gently to combine. Cover and refrigerate for 1 hour before serving.

tomato sauce

serves 4

Serve with hamburgers, sausages, steaks, fish or steamed vegetables.

1 tablespoon olive oil

20 g (3/4 oz) butter

1 small onion, finely chopped

1 garlic clove, crushed

1–2 teaspoons Italian dried mixed herbs

2 large tomatoes, chopped

125 ml (4 fl oz/1/2 cup) tomato passata (puréed tomatoes)

2 teaspoons balsamic vinegar

1 Heat the oil and butter in a small saucepan. Add the onion, garlic and mixed herbs and cook for 2–3 minutes, or until the onion is soft.

2 Stir in the tomatoes, tomato passata and vinegar and cook for 3–4 minutes. Set aside to cool slightly.

3 Process the tomato mixture in a food processor until smooth. Season to taste with salt and freshly ground black pepper. Serve warm or cold.

velouté sauce

serves 4

Serve with grilled (broiled) chicken, seafood or veal.

30 g (1 oz) butter

30 g (1 oz/¼ cup) plain (all-purpose) flour

375 ml (13 fl oz/1½ cups) chicken, fish or veal stock

lemon juice, to taste

1 tablespoon cream (whipping)

1 Melt the butter in a saucepan over medium heat, add the flour and cook, without browning, for 2 minutes, or until a thick paste has formed.

2 Whisk in the stock a little at a time to prevent the mixture from becoming lumpy. Cook, whisking continuously, for 3–5 minutes, or until the sauce is quite thick and doesn't have a floury taste.

3 Season to taste with salt, freshly ground black pepper and lemon juice, adding a little at a time. Stir in the cream and serve immediately, as the sauce will quickly thicken. If necessary, add a little extra stock to thin it down.

Melt the butter in a pan and cook the flour until it bubbles and thickens.

Whisk in the stock a little at a time to prevent lumps forming.

Add the lemon juice a little at a time, tasting after each addition.

vinaigrette (French dressing)

serves 4

Serve drizzled over a green salad.

2 tablespoons white
wine vinegar

80 ml (2¹/₂ fl oz/¹/₃ cup)
light olive oil

1 teaspoon Dijon mustard

1　Whisk the vinegar, olive oil and mustard in a small bowl until combined. Season with salt and freshly ground black pepper and whisk until well blended.

yakitori sauce

serves 6

Brush the sauce over chicken or fish skewers as they are cooking.

125 ml (4 fl oz/¹/₂ cup) sake

125 ml (4 fl oz/¹/₂ cup) mirin

185 ml (6 fl oz/³/₄ cup)
Japanese soy sauce

2 tablespoons sugar

1　Put the sake, mirin, soy sauce and sugar in a saucepan and stir over low heat until the sugar has dissolved. Bring to the boil, then remove from the heat.

wasabi mayonnaise

serves 4

Serve with chicken or seafood.

125 g (4^1/$_2$ oz/^{1}/$_2$ cup)
whole-egg mayonnaise

1 teaspoon wasabi paste

2 teaspoons Japanese
soy sauce

1 Put the mayonnaise, wasabi paste and soy sauce
in a small bowl and stir to combine. Cover and
refrigerate until ready to serve.

zucchini, ricotta and Parmesan sauce

serves 4

Serve with pasta.

2 zucchini (courgettes), chopped

2 garlic cloves, chopped

1 small red chilli, seeded and chopped

125 g (4¹/2 oz/¹/2 cup) ricotta cheese

100 ml (3¹/2 fl oz) pouring cream

2 teaspoons finely grated lemon zest

100 g (3¹/2 oz/1 cup) grated Parmesan cheese

1 handful basil, chopped

Parmesan cheese shavings, to serve

1 Put the zucchini, garlic and chilli in a small processor fitted with the metal blade and whizz in short bursts for 30 seconds, or until finely chopped.

2 Add the ricotta, cream, lemon zest, Parmesan and chopped basil, and season well with salt and freshly ground black pepper. Whizz for 20 seconds, or until smooth. Serve with Parmesan shavings. Prepare this sauce just prior to serving. It is not suitable for freezing.

sweet sauces

apricot liqueur sauce

serves 6

125 g (4½ oz/⅔ cup) dried apricots, roughly chopped

250 ml (9 fl oz/1 cup) apple juice

3 wide strips lemon zest, white pith removed

55 g (2 oz/¼ cup) sugar

1 tablespoon Cointreau or other orange liqueur, optional

Serve with steamed puddings.

1 Put the apricots, apple juice, lemon zest and 250 ml (9 fl oz/1 cup) of water in a saucepan. Bring to the boil, then reduce the heat and simmer, partially covered, for 10 minutes, or until the apricots are tender. Remove the lemon zest.

2 Add the sugar and stir until it has dissolved completely. Set aside to cool for 10 minutes.

3 Transfer the apricot mixture to a food processor and process until smooth. Stir in the liqueur, if using.

berry coulis

serves 6

250 g (9 oz/2 cups) mixed berries, such as strawberries, raspberries and blackberries

2–4 tablespoons icing (confectioners') sugar, or to taste

1 tablespoon lemon juice

1–2 tablespoons Cointreau or other orange liqueur, optional

Serve with fresh or poached fruit, soufflés, ice cream, sorbet, pies and tarts.

1 Hull the berries and place in a food processor.

2 Add the sugar and lemon juice and process until smooth. Stir in the liqueur, if using.

Hull the berries (remove the stalks and leaves from the fruit).

Put the fruit in a food processor or blender with the sugar and lemon juice.

Stir the liqueur into the blended coulis, adding as much or as little as you like.

blackberry sauce

serves 4

Serve with mousse or vanilla ice cream.

150 g (5¹/2 oz/1¹/4 cups) blackberries

80 ml (2¹/2 fl oz/¹/3 cup) red wine

2 tablespoons caster (superfine) sugar

1 teaspoon cornflour(cornstarch)

1 Put the blackberries, wine and sugar in a small saucepan. Stir over low heat until the sugar has dissolved, pressing the berries with the back of a spoon, then simmer for 2 minutes.

2 Blend the cornflour with 2 teaspoons of water, add to the saucepan and stir until the mixture boils and thickens. Strain the sauce to remove the seeds. Set aside to cool before serving.

blueberry sauce

serves 6

Serve with ice cream or pancakes.

500 g (1 lb 2 oz/3¹/4 cups) blueberries

2 tablespoons balsamic vinegar

55 g (2 oz/¹/4 cup) caster (superfine) sugar

1 Combine the blueberries and vinegar in a non-metallic bowl and set aside for 30 minutes to macerate the fruit.

2 Transfer the blueberry mixture to a saucepan and add the sugar. Stir over low heat until the sugar has dissolved. Bring to the boil, then reduce the heat and simmer for 2–3 minutes. Serve warm.

brandy cream sauce

serves 12

Serve with plum pudding or chocolate steamed pudding, fresh or poached fruit or fruit pies.

2 eggs, separated

80 g (2³/₄ oz/¹/₃ cup) caster (superfine) sugar

80 ml (2¹/₂ fl oz/¹/₃ cup) brandy

250 ml (9 fl oz/1 cup) cream (whipping), lightly whipped

1 Beat the egg yolks and sugar until the mixture is thick and creamy and the sugar has dissolved. Stir in the brandy and fold in the cream.

2 Beat the egg whites in a small bowl until soft peaks form. Fold into the sauce and serve immediately.

Beat together the egg yolks and sugar until thick and creamy.

Lightly fold in the whipped cream, using a metal spoon.

Beat the egg whites and then fold into the sauce, trying to keep the volume.

brandy custard

serves 6-8

Serve with plum pudding or steamed puddings.

3 egg yolks

115 g (4 oz/1/2 cup) caster (superfine) sugar

1 tablespoon custard powder

250 ml (9 fl oz/1 cup) milk

250 ml (9 fl oz/1 cup) cream (whipping)

2 tablespoons brandy

1 Whisk the egg yolks, sugar and custard powder in a bowl.

2 Combine the milk and cream in a saucepan and heat until just boiling. Gradually pour onto the egg yolk mixture, whisking continuously.

3 Transfer the mixture to the saucepan and stir over low heat for 5 minutes, or until the custard has thickened. Stir in the brandy. Serve warm.

burnt sugar sauce

serves 6

440 g (15¹/₂ oz/2 cups) sugar

Serve with waffles and ice cream, pancakes or crepes. Also good with fresh or poached fruit.

1   Mix the sugar and 250 ml (9 fl oz/1 cup) of water in a deep saucepan. Stir over low heat, without boiling, until the sugar has dissolved. Increase the heat and bring to the boil. Brush down the side of the pan with a pastry brush dipped in water to prevent sugar crystals from forming. Reduce the heat and simmer, without stirring, until the mixture turns dark brown and begins to smell burnt.

2   Put a tea towel in the sink to stand the pan on (the sink may buckle if it is not protected). Transfer the pan to the sink, place a tea towel over your arm to protect it and add 185 ml (6 fl oz/³/₄ cup) of water to the pan. The mixture will splutter violently. When the spluttering subsides, return the pan to medium heat and stir with a wooden spoon until the caramel dissolves and comes to the boil. Reduce the heat and simmer for 1 minute.

3   Set aside in the pan to cool, then pour into an airtight container and refrigerate overnight for the sauce to thicken.

butterscotch sauce

serves 6

125 g (4¹/₂ oz) butter

90 g (3¹/₄ oz/¹/₂ cup) soft brown sugar

2 tablespoons golden syrup (see note)

125 ml (4 fl oz/¹/₂ cup) cream (whipping)

1 teaspoon natural vanilla extract

Serve with grilled (broiled) bananas, peaches or nectarines, fresh fruit, steamed puddings, waffles or crepes.

1 Put the butter and brown sugar in a saucepan and stir over low heat until the butter has melted and the sugar has dissolved.

2 Bring to the boil and add the golden syrup and cream. Reduce the heat and simmer for 10 minutes, or until the sauce has thickened slightly. Remove from the heat and add the vanilla. Serve hot or cold.

Note: If preferred, reduce the butter to 60 g (2¹/₄ oz) and omit the golden syrup.

Put the butter and sugar in a pan and stir over low heat until dissolved.

Add the syrup and cream to the pan and simmer for 10 minutes.

Remove the sauce from the heat and stir in the vanilla essence.

caramel rum sauce

serves 6

Serve on steamed puddings or ice cream.

225 g (8 oz/1 cup) caster (superfine) sugar

200 ml (7 fl oz) thick (double/heavy) cream

50 g (1³/4 oz) butter

2 tablespoons dark rum

1 Put the sugar and 150 ml (5 fl oz) of water in a saucepan and stir until the sugar has dissolved. Bring to the boil and continue to boil until golden brown.

2 Remove from the heat and add the cream. Re-dissolve any lumps, then add the butter and rum. Stir until smooth. Serve warm.

cherry sauce

serves 4

Serve with waffles and ice cream or chocolate cake.

3 x 425 g (15 oz) tins pitted black cherries

115 g (4 oz/¹/2 cup) caster (superfine) sugar

1 vanilla bean, split lengthways

1 cinnamon stick

2 star anise

1 Drain the cherries, reserving 170 ml (5¹/2 fl oz/²/3 cup) of the syrup. Put the cherries, syrup, sugar, vanilla bean, cinnamon stick and star anise in a saucepan.

2 Simmer, stirring occasionally, for 25 minutes, or until the sugar has dissolved and the sauce is thick and syrupy. Remove the vanilla bean, cinnamon stick and star anise. Serve warm or cold.

caramel sauce

serves 6

Serve with ice cream, pancakes, steamed puddings or cakes.

225 g (8 oz/1 cup) caster (superfine) sugar

125 ml (4 fl oz/1/2 cup) of hot water

400 g (14 oz) condensed milk

1 tablespoon golden syrup, optional

1 teaspoon natural vanilla extract

1 Put the sugar and 60 ml (2 fl oz/1/4 cup) of water in a small heavy-based saucepan. Stir over low heat, without boiling, for 10 minutes, or until the sugar has dissolved. Brush any crystals from the side of the pan with a wet pastry brush.

2 Increase the heat to medium and simmer, without stirring, until the mixture turns a deep caramel colour. Remove from the heat and, using a tea towel to protect your hands, slowly and carefully pour on the hot water. The caramel will spit when the hot water is added, so take care.

3 Return the saucepan to low heat and stir until the caramel has melted again. Remove from the heat and stir in the condensed milk, golden syrup, if using, and vanilla. Serve warm or chilled. The sauce will thicken when refrigerated.

chocolate cherry sauce

serves 6

425 g (15 oz) tin pitted
black cherries

100 ml (3¹/₂ fl oz)
cream (whipping)

200 g (7 oz/1¹/₃ cups)
chopped dark chocolate

Serve with pancakes and ice cream.

1 Drain the cherries, reserving 2 tablespoons of the syrup.

2 Put the cream and chocolate in a heatproof bowl. Bring a saucepan of water to the boil, then remove from the heat. Sit the bowl over the pan, making sure the base of the bowl does not touch the water. Stir occasionally until the chocolate has melted and combined with the cream.

3 Stir the cherries and reserved syrup into the chocolate mixture. Serve warm.

chocolate fudge sauce

serves 8

250 g (9 oz/1²/₃ cups) chopped good-quality dark chocolate

185 ml (6 fl oz/³/₄ cup) cream (whipping)

50 g (1³/₄ oz) butter

1 tablespoon golden syrup or corn syrup

2 tablespoons Baileys, Tia Maria or Kahlúa

Serve with ice cream, profiteroles, waffles, pancakes, poached fruit or steamed puddings.

1 Place the chocolate, cream, butter and golden syrup or corn syrup in a saucepan. Stir over low heat until the chocolate has melted and the mixture is smooth.

2 Stir in the liqueur. Serve hot or cold.

chocolate orange sauce

serves 8

Serve over profiteroles or ice cream.

3 large strips orange zest,
white pith removed

125 ml (4 fl oz/1/2 cup)
orange juice

2 tablespoons caster
(superfine) sugar

200 g (7 oz/1 1/3 cups)
chopped milk chocolate

300 ml (10 1/2 fl oz)
cream (whipping)

2 teaspoons Cointreau or
other orange liqueur

1   Put the orange zest and orange juice in a small
    saucepan and bring to the boil. Stir in the sugar, then
    simmer for 3 minutes, or until the mixture is thick and
    syrupy and reduced to 2 tablespoons. Set aside to cool,
    then cut the zest into thin strips.

2   Put the chocolate in a heatproof bowl. Bring the cream
    to the boil, then pour it over the chocolate and set
    aside for 2 minutes. Stir until the chocolate has
    melted, then stir in the orange syrup, orange zest and
    liqueur. Serve warm.

citrus syrup

serves 8

Serve over hot or cold cake.

350 g (12 oz/1¹/₂ cups) caster (superfine) sugar

3 strips citrus zest, white pith removed

80 ml (2¹/₂ fl oz/¹/₃ cup) lemon, lime, orange or mandarin juice

1 Put the sugar, zest, juice and 80 ml (2¹/₂fl oz/¹/₃ cup) of water in a saucepan. Stir over low heat, without boiling, until the sugar has dissolved.

2 Bring to the boil, then reduce the heat and simmer for 12–15 minutes, or until the syrup has slightly thickened. Remove the zest before serving. Serve warm or cold.

coconut lime anglaise

serves 4

Serve with steamed puddings, poached fruit or jelly desserts.

3 egg yolks

55 g (2 oz/$\frac{1}{4}$ cup) caster (superfine) sugar

1 teaspoon cornflour (cornstarch)

185 ml (6 fl oz/$\frac{3}{4}$ cup) coconut cream

125 ml (4 fl oz/$\frac{1}{2}$ cup) milk

60 ml (2 fl oz/$\frac{1}{4}$ cup) cream (whipping)

1 teaspoon finely grated lime zest

1 Whisk the egg yolks, sugar and cornflour in a heatproof bowl with electric beaters until light and creamy.

2 Put the coconut cream, milk, cream and lime zest in a small saucepan and heat until almost boiling, then pour onto the egg mixture, beating constantly.

3 Return the mixture to the saucepan and stir over low heat for about 5 minutes, or until slightly thickened — do not allow the sauce to boil or it will curdle.

4 Strain the sauce into a chilled heatproof bowl and serve immediately, or cover the surface with plastic wrap to prevent a skin forming and serve cold.

Whisk together the egg yolks, caster sugar and cornflour.

Pour the hot mixture onto the egg mixture, whisking continuously.

Strain the sauce into the chilled bowl or jug and serve immediately, or cover.

coffee anglaise

serves 4-6

Serve over steamed puddings, dessert muffins or mousse.

2 egg yolks

2 tablespoons caster (superfine) sugar

250 ml (9 fl oz/1 cup) milk

1 1/2 teaspoons instant coffee granules

1 Beat the egg yolks and sugar in a mixing bowl until light and creamy.

2 Put the milk and coffee granules in a saucepan and stir over medium heat until the coffee has dissolved. Bring to the boil, then remove from the heat and gradually whisk in the egg yolk mixture.

3 Stir constantly over low heat for 5 minutes, or until the mixture coats the back of a spoon — do not allow the sauce to boil or it will curdle.

4 Remove the pan from the heat and transfer the sauce to a bowl. Serve immediately, or cover the surface with plastic wrap to prevent a skin forming and serve cold.

créme anglaise

Serve with fruit pastries, warm cakes or steamed puddings.

3 egg yolks

2 tablespoons caster (superfine) sugar

375 ml (13 fl oz/1¹/₂ cups) milk

¹/₂ teaspoon natural vanilla extract

1 Whisk the egg yolks and sugar in a heatproof bowl for 2 minutes, or until light and creamy. Heat the milk in a small saucepan until almost boiling, then pour onto the egg mixture, whisking constantly.

2 Return the mixture to the pan and stir over low heat for about 5 minutes, or until slightly thickened, enough to coat the back of a spoon. Do not allow the custard to boil or it will curdle.

3 Remove the pan from the heat and stir in the vanilla. Transfer the sauce to a bowl and serve immediately, or cover the surface with plastic wrap to prevent a skin forming and serve cold.

Whisk together the egg yolks and sugar in a bowl.

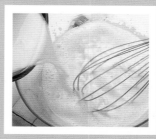

Place the bowl on a tea towel to prevent it slipping as you whisk.

Cover the surface of the custard with plastic wrap to stop it forming a skin.

hard sauce

serves 8

Serve with plum pudding.

125 g (4¹/₂ oz) unsalted
butter

250 g (9 oz/2 cups) sifted icing
(confectioners') sugar

1 tablespoon brandy, whisky
or rum

1 Beat the butter in a bowl until soft. Gradually
add the icing sugar and beat until the mixture is
light and creamy.

2 Beat in the brandy, whisky or rum. Cover and
refrigerate until firm.

jam sauce

serves 8

Serve with ice cream and warm cakes or
steamed puddings.

310 g (11 oz/1 cup) jam

1 teaspoon finely grated
lemon zest

caster (superfine) sugar,
to taste

1 Combine the jam, lemon zest and 250 ml (9 fl oz/1
cup) of water in a small saucepan. Stir over medium
heat, then reduce the heat slightly and bring to
the boil.

2 Reduce the heat and simmer for 10 minutes. Stir
in the sugar, to taste. Serve warm.

lemon and lime sauce

serves 4-6

225 g (8 oz/1 cup) caster (superfine) sugar

60 ml (2 fl oz/¼ cup) lemon juice

60 ml (2 fl oz/¼ cup) lime juice

2 tablespoons vodka

1 tablespoon chopped mint

zest of 1 lemon, white pith removed, cut into fine strips

Serve over fresh fruit such as sliced oranges, or use as a poaching liquid for fruit.

1   Put the sugar, lemon juice, lime juice and 250 ml (9 fl oz/1 cup) of water in a saucepan. Stir over low heat until the sugar has dissolved. Slowly bring to the boil, then reduce the heat and simmer, without stirring, until the mixture has thickened to a syrupy consistency.

2   Remove the pan from the heat, stir in the vodka and set aside to cool.

3   Add the mint and strips of lemon zest and pour into a sterilized jar. Store the sauce in the refrigerator for up to two weeks.

lime curd

2 tablespoons lime juice

60 g (2¼ oz) unsalted butter, melted

40 g (1½ oz) icing sugar

1 egg yolk

Serve with fruit pastries, warm cakes or steamed puddings.

1 Place the lime juice, butter and sifted icing sugar in a small saucepan, and heat to a simmer, stirring until all the sugar has dissolved.

2 Remove from the heat and cool slightly, then whisk in the reserved egg yolk.

3 Return to very low heat and stir for 5 minutes, or until thickened. Do not boil.

praline cream sauce

serves 6

80 g (2³/₄ oz/¹/₂ cup) roasted
blanched almonds

115 g (4 oz/¹/₂ cup) caster
(superfine) sugar

100 g (3¹/₂ oz/¹/₃ cup)
chocolate hazelnut spread

300 ml (10¹/₂ fl oz)
cream (whipping)

Serve with fresh or poached fruit, pancakes, crepes or chocolate cake.

1 Arrange the almonds in a single layer on a lined baking tray.

2 Combine the sugar with 80 ml (2¹/₂ fl oz/¹/₃ cup) of water in a small saucepan. Stir over low heat, without boiling, until the sugar has dissolved. Cook, without stirring, until the mixture turns golden, then quickly pour it over the almonds. Allow to set until hard, then process the praline in a food processor until it is broken into fine crumbs.

3 Put the hazelnut spread in a heatproof bowl over a saucepan of hot water until the spread softens slightly. Remove the bowl from the pan and stir in the cream. Whisk until smooth (do not overbeat or the sauce will become grainy), then fold in the praline crumbs and serve.

raisin butterscotch sauce

serves 6

Serve with ice cream.

2 tablespoons brandy

40 g (1¹/2 oz/¹/3 cup) raisins

80 ml (2¹/2fl oz/¹/3 cup)
cream (whipping)

60 g (2¹/4 oz) butter, cubed

50 g (1³/4 oz/1/4 cup) soft
brown sugar

1 Put the brandy and raisins in a small saucepan and stir over medium heat for 5 minutes. Transfer to a bowl.

2 Put the cream, butter and brown sugar in the same saucepan and stir until the sugar begins to dissolve and the butter begins to melt. Bring to the boil, then reduce the heat and simmer for 5 minutes, or until the mixture thickens slightly. Pour into the bowl with the brandied raisins and mix well. Serve warm.

raspberry coulis

serves 8

Serve with ice cream, sorbet or cheesecake.

300 g (10¹/2 oz/2¹/2 cups)
raspberries

30 g (1 oz/¹/4 cup) icing
(confectioners') sugar

1 Process the raspberries and sugar in a food processor for 20 seconds, or until smooth. Add the lemon juice, to taste.

strawberry sauce

serves 6-8

Serve with fruit fritters or ice cream.

55 g (2 oz/¼ cup) caster (superfine) sugar

250 g (9 oz/1²/₃ cups) strawberries

2 tablespoons brandy or strawberry liqueur

1 Put the sugar and 60 ml (2 fl oz/¼ cup) of water in a saucepan and heat until the sugar has dissolved. Add the strawberries and simmer for 5 minutes. Remove from the heat and set aside to cool slightly.

2 Process the strawberry mixture in a food processor for 30 seconds, or until smooth. Stir in the brandy, to taste. Serve warm or cold.

vanilla custard

serves 6

Serve with sweet pies, pastries or steamed puddings.

250 ml (9 fl oz/1 cup) milk

60 ml (2 fl oz/¼ cup) cream (whipping)

3 egg yolks

80 g (2¾ oz/⅓ cup) caster (superfine) sugar

2 teaspoons cornflour (cornstarch)

1 teaspoon natural vanilla extract

1 Put the milk and cream in a saucepan and bring to the boil. Immediately remove the pan from the heat.

2 Whisk the egg yolks, sugar and cornflour in a heatproof bowl. Slowly pour the hot milk mixture over the egg mixture, whisking continuously.

3 Return the mixture to the saucepan and stir over low heat, without boiling, for 5 minutes, or until the custard starts to bubble and thicken. Remove from the heat immediately. Whisk in the vanilla and serve warm.

Whisk the egg yolks with the sugar and cornflour in a heatproof bowl.

Place the bowl on a tea towel to stop it slipping while you whisk in the hot milk.

Remove the pan from the heat and whisk in the vanilla.

zabaglione

serves 10-12

8 egg yolks

80 g (2³/4 oz/¹/3 cup) caster (superfine) sugar

310 ml (10³/4 fl oz/1¹/4 cups) sweet Marsala

Serve with savoiardi (lady fingers), fresh berries, poached or grilled (broiled) fruits.

1 Beat the egg yolks and sugar in a heatproof bowl with electric beaters until pale yellow.

2 Put the bowl over a gently simmering pan of water and beat continuously, adding the Marsala gradually. Beat for 5 minutes, or until thick and frothy. To test if it is ready, dip a metal spoon into the sauce and hold it up — if the mixture slides down the back it is not yet thickened enough. If you can draw a line through the sauce with a spoon and leave a trail, it is ready. Serve immediately or serve chilled.

Beat the egg yolks and sugar with electric beaters until pale yellow.

Place the bowl over a pan of simmering water. Add the Marsala as you beat.

When the Zabaglione leaves a trail from a spoon, it is ready to serve.